faiThGirLz!™

chickChat

more Devotions for Girls

D0067247

Written by Kristi Holl
with Jennifer Vogtlin

ZONDERkidz

ZONDERVAN.com/
AUTHORTRACKER
follow your favorite authors

Also by Kristi Holl

No Boys Allowed
What's a Girl to Do?
Girlz Rock
Chick Chat
Shine on, Girl!

Boarding School Mysteries

Vanished (Book One)
Betrayed (Book Two)
Burned (Book Three)
Poisoned (Book Four)

Other books in the growing Faithgirlz!™ library

Bibles

The Faithgirlz! Bible
NIV Faithgirlz! Backpack Bible

Faithgirlz! Bible Studies

Secret Power of Love
Secret Power of Joy
Secret Power of Goodness
Secret Power of Grace

Fiction

From Sadie's Sketchbook

Shades of Truth (Book One)
Flickering Hope (Book Two)
Waves of Light (Book Three)
Brilliant Hues (Book Four)

Sophie's World Series

Meet Sophie (Book One)
Sophie Steps Up (Book Two)
Sophie and Friends (Book Three)
Sophie's Friendship Fiasco (Book Four)
Sophie Flakes Out (Book Five)
Sophie's Drama (Book Six)

The Lucy Series

Lucy Doesn't Wear Pink (Book One)
Lucy Out of Bounds (Book Two)
Lucy's Perfect Summer (Book Three)
Lucy Finds Her Way (Book Four)

The Girls of Harbor View

Girl Power (Book One)
Take Charge (Book Two)
Raising Faith (Book Three)
Secret Admirer (Book Four)

Nonfiction

Faithgirlz Handbook
Faithgirlz Journal
Food, Faith, and Fun! Faithgirlz Cookbook
Real Girls of the Bible
My Beautiful Daughter
You! A Christian Girl's Guide to Growing Up
Girl Politics
Everybody Tells Me to Be Myslef, but I Don't Know Who I Am

Check out www.faithgirlz.com

ZONDERKIDZ

Chick Chat
Text copyright © 2006 by Kristi Holl

Requests for information should be addressed to:
Zonderkidz, *Grand Rapids, Michigan 49530*

Library of Congress Cataloging-in-Publication Data

Holl, Kristi.
    Chick chat : more devotions for girls / by Kristi Holl with Jennifer Vogtlin.
      p. cm. — (Faithgirlz)
    ISBN: 978-0-310-71143-8 (softcover)
      1. Girls—Prayer-books and devotions—English. I. Vogtlin, Jennifer, 1976- II. Title. III. Series.
BV4860.H6 2006
242'.62—dc22   2005033613

Art direction: Jody Langley
Interior design: Susan Ambs
Interior composition: Ruth Bandstra
Cover design: Sarah Molegraaf
Illustrated by: Robin Zingone

Printed in the United States

QG 10-26-15

13 14 15 16 17 18 19 20 /QVS/ 26 25 24 23 22 21 20 19 18 17 16 15 14 13 12 11 10 9

Contents

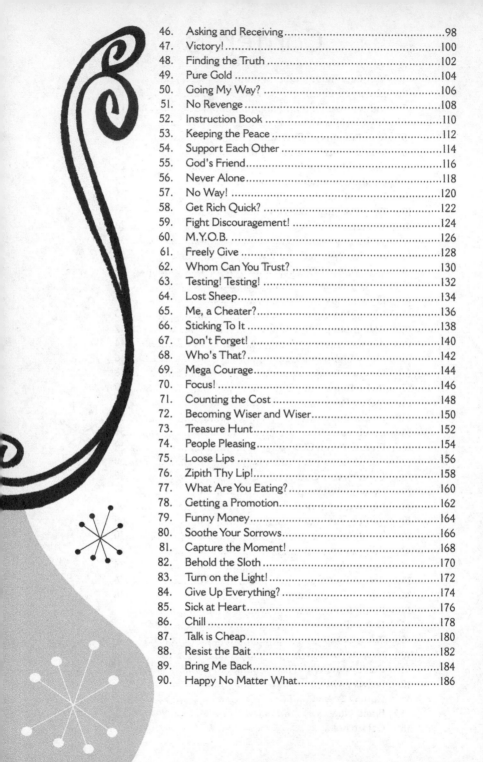

So we fix our eyes not on what is seen, but on what is unseen. For what is seen is temporary, but what is unseen is eternal.

–2 Corinthians 4:18

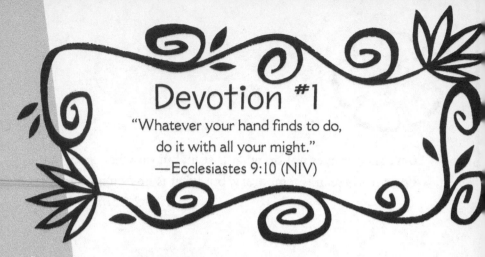

Devotion #1

"Whatever your hand finds to do,
do it with all your might."
—Ecclesiastes 9:10 (NIV)

Your Best Shot

On different days, you do different jobs with your hands: wash dishes, shovel snow, do math problems, practice cheerleading routines, clean your room—and so much more. Instead of rushing through each activity, do your very best work. Don't just do enough to get by.

That sounds inspiring, but what if the job is something you don't understand? What if it's a task to do for someone who irritates you, like your bossy big brother? What if you're paired for a science project with a rude girl with scraggly hair who actually wears pink boots in the classroom? You don't want to go the extra mile. In fact, you're willing to take an F for the project if the science teacher will let you off the hook. That isn't going to happen, so you grit your teeth and get to work with her.

Then one day you learn a great secret from Colossians 3:23 (NLT): "Work hard and cheerfully at whatever you do, as though you were working for the Lord rather than for people." Each day after that, when you walk into science class, you take a deep breath and say, "You know I don't want to do this, Lord, but I'm doing it for you." Then, with a fresh surge of energy, you work with all your strength.

Whatever you have to do today—whether it's stuff you love or stuff you hate—do it to the very best of your ability. Be determined. There is much satisfaction to be found in a job well done.

Did You Know ...

one way to show love to others is to "never be lazy in your work, but serve the Lord enthusiastically." Romans 12:11 NLT

More To Explore: 1 Corinthians 15:10

GirL TaLk:

What activities, school subjects, or chores are the hardest for you to do "with all your might"? If you performed them with excellence, might you feel differently about them?

God TaLk:

Lord, I want to do everything to the best of my ability. Help me to remember that I'm really doing it all for you. Amen

FuN FaCToid:

Exercise with all your might too! A one-hundred-pound, twelve-year-old girl biking leisurely (under ten miles per hour) burns 181 calories in an hour. But by biking vigorously with all her strength (between sixteen and nineteen miles per hour), that same girl can burn 544 calories per hour!

Devotion #2

"A friend is always loyal, and a brother is born to help in time of need."—Proverbs 17:17 (NLT)

Loyalty

A friend loves at *all* times. She shows unwavering devotion to others and is truehearted. A real friend keeps the promises she makes. Close friends are there to help when sudden suffering, distress, or trouble strikes.

Anna was worried about her best friend, Jessie. Jessie's dad had been arrested for taking money from the company where he worked. Jessie was afraid to go to school, fearing the remarks other kids were sure to make. The week after the arrest report appeared in the newspaper, many of her classmates *did* make nasty or thoughtless remarks. But Anna stuck by Jessie, never leaving her side before school or during lunch or on the way home. She stuck up for her, shielded her from nosy questions, and (most important) prayed for her and her family situation. "A man who has friends must himself be friendly, but there is a friend who sticks closer than a brother" (Proverbs 18:24 NKJV).

You may have brothers within your family circle at home. But if you are a believer, you have *many* brothers (and sisters)—others who also love the Lord. You need to be loyal to them. The friend you must be most loyal to is Jesus. He said to his disciples, "Greater love has no one than this: to lay down one's life for one's friends. You are my friends if you do what I command" (John 15:13–14 TNIV).

You are never without friends. Jesus is your best friend, and he will stick closer to you than anyone else can. What a privilege it is to have such a friend!

Did You Know ...

Jonathan was such a good friend to David that he made a special vow to David, and he sealed the pact by giving David his robe, tunic, sword, bow, and belt? See 1 Samuel 18:3–4.

More To Explore: Ruth 1:16–17

Girl Talk:

Can you think of a friend who has helped you through some trouble? What friends have *you* helped through a tough time?

God Talk:

Father, thank you for giving me good friends. Help me be a loyal friend to others. Amen.

Mini Quiz:

Are you a loyal friend? Your best friend's been feeling down. You

A. invite her to spend the night so you can talk through her problems.

B. call her to ask what's wrong.

C. tell her to snap out of it!

(Answer: A. Loyalty Plus!; B. average; C. zero)

Devotion #3

"God blesses the people who patiently endure testing.
Afterward they will receive the crown of life that
God has promised to those who love him."
—James 1:12 (NLT)

Victory Prize

People who do God's will during times of trial and testing are blessed and happy. Afterward they will receive the "crown of life," or eternal life. In biblical times, a crown was a wreath placed on the head of a victorious athlete.

You may be an athlete, but you may not feel victorious! You may be exhausted. When you join the track team, you dream of getting in shape and winning a ribbon at the first meet. However, a week into the season you want to quit. Your shins hurt. Your ribs ache. Your lungs burn. Your big toes are bruised. And yet, you want that ribbon.

So you take a deep breath and head out to run those laps.

Ribbons aren't given simply for entering the race. Prizes aren't awarded for merely entering your art project in the contest. Diplomas aren't given just for starting high school. Starting isn't difficult.

You also need to *patiently endure* a testing time before receiving the award. Note: Going through a test with grumbling and complaining will *not* result in being blessed by God. Awards are given to those who "keep on keeping on" when they'd rather quit—plus they strive to finish the job with a good attitude. "As you know, we consider blessed those who have persevered" (James 5:11 NIV).

If you're a follower of Jesus, you have the power of God inside you. You can't overcome problems by yourself, but the Holy Spirit working through you can!

Did You Know ...

Abraham was tested for many *years* after receiving an important promise from God? But he waited patiently—and in time received what God had promised. See Hebrews 6:15.

Girl Talk:

What trial or test are you facing right now? A financial problem? A relationship test at school or home? A health issue? Do you grumble and complain—or do you still have the joy of the Lord?

More To Explore: James 1:2–4 and 1 Corinthians 9:25

God Talk:

Lord, I can't win without your help, but help me to also do my part to be patient and endure. I won't quit! Amen.

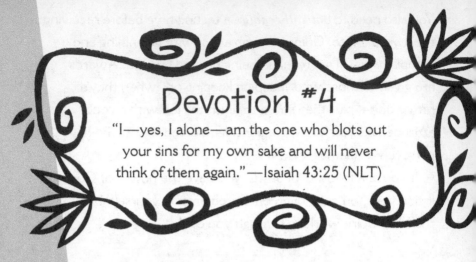

Devotion #4

"I—yes, I alone—am the one who blots out your sins for my own sake and will never think of them again."—Isaiah 43:25 (NLT)

Gone and Forgotten

When we do something wrong, only God can deal with our sins. To show his mercy and love, he forgives them. He even chooses never to think of those sins again. They're totally wiped out!

Nicole forgot her math book and ran back to the classroom after school to get it. No one was there. Crossing the room, she spotted a wadded-up five-dollar bill and picked it up. It must have fallen out of someone's pocket, Nicole reasoned. There was no way to tell who the money belonged to. "Finders, keepers," she muttered, stuffing it in her pants pocket.

Halfway home, Nicole began to feel guilty, as if she had THIEF tattooed on her forehead. She knew she should have turned the money in to the office or left it on the teacher's desk. It wasn't "finders, keepers." It was stealing. "Lord, I'm sorry," she prayed. "I shouldn't have taken the money."

Nicole headed back to the school, where

she turned the money into the principal's office. She still felt guilty, though, until she read Jeremiah 31:34 (NLT): "And I will forgive their wickedness and will never again remember their sins." Nicole decided that if God could forgive and forget her wrongdoings, then she would shake off that feeling and forget it too.

God isn't waiting to punish you the minute you do something wrong. When you confess, God forgives your sins completely. It's over and done with. God chooses to wipe it from his memory—and you can forget it too.

Did You Know ...

God made a new covenant (or promise) with his people, an awesome promise that included to never again remember our sins? See Hebrews 8:7–12.

More To Explore: Joel 2:13–14

Girl Talk:

Have you done something this week that you feel guilty about? Is there something you can do about it—right now?

God Talk:

Lord, I choose to do wrong things every day. Please forgive me for _____. Thank you for forgiving and forgetting. Amen.

Fun Factoid:

The ability of the human brain to remember is virtually limitless. It was estimated that the number of patterns nerve cells could form and remember was 1 followed by 800 zeros!

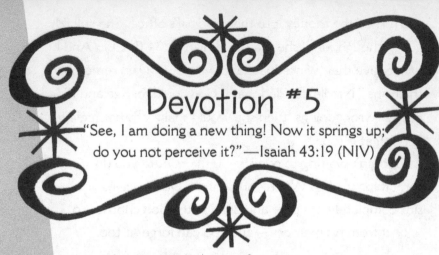

Devotion #5

"See, I am doing a new thing! Now it springs up; do you not perceive it?"—Isaiah 43:19 (NIV)

IT's a Brand-New Day!

We get used to doing things the same old way, day after day, month after month, and year after year. We get stuck in ruts, but often God wants to do a *new* thing in our lives. The "new thing" might be a change in behavior with family or friends, a school activity to start (or drop), or a new after-school job. When it "springs up," we need to pay attention to it.

Suppose your friends are all on the volleyball team, but you want to join the school's new video production team. It sounds exciting—but it meets after school when the volleyball team practices. It takes courage for you to tell your friends you're dropping volleyball this year to join the video production team. You know you'll miss your friends after school. Yet, the new project excites you, and you hope you'll make even more friends as you work to produce the school's daily news reports. It's up to you to branch out and try new things. "Each of you must take responsibility for doing the creative best you can with your own life" (Galatians 6:5 MSG).

God is always in the process of doing new things in your life. He wants you to think creatively and use your imagination to experiment with fresh ideas. We must be willing to take some risks (and even fail a few times) on the way to success.

Don't be afraid to try new things: new activities, new attitudes, and new relationships. Branch out and see what wonderful things God has in store for you!

Did You Know ...

hobbies can be new and creative? Try making candy with a volcano that erupts gooey chocolate that runs into built-in molds. Or get a Meteor Maker, which shines constellations and streaking comets on your ceiling.

More To Explore: Isaiah 42:9

Girl Talk:

Are you stuck in routines that never change? What new hobby or activity could you try this week? What person at school could you talk to for the first time?

God Talk:

Lord, you are so creative. I know you want to do many new things in my life, both now and as I grow up. Give me courage to take some risks. Amen.

Devotion #6

"Forsake not [Wisdom], and she will keep, defend, *and* protect you; love her, and she will guard you . . . Prize Wisdom highly *and* exalt her, and she will exalt *and* promote you; she will bring you to honor when you embrace her."
—Proverbs 4:6, 8 (AMP)

Win The Prize!

Wisdom is the ability to apply knowledge, experience, and good sense to your life. Wisdom from God is sensible and shows sound judgment. So don't abandon wisdom! Wisdom will protect you against attack and shield you from danger and destruction. Value wisdom highly and make it your primary goal.

Maria felt her mom was too old-fashioned about money. She lectured Maria about staying within her budget, saving for things she wanted, babysitting to pay for extras, and turning down her friends when she couldn't afford to go to movies. Maria figured her mom had forgotten what it was like to be young, so she ignored the advice.

After her allowance was gone, she spent the money given to her for school supplies. When that ran out, she borrowed from her friends. She turned down babysitting jobs on the weekends to go with friends to the mall. Eventually, though, Maria wondered if her mom was more wise than old-fashioned. Maria's friends demanded what she owed them. They were mad that she couldn't repay them, as she'd promised. The neighbors stopped calling her for jobs and found someone else they could depend on. Embarrassed, Maria explained to her teachers why she still didn't have the right school supplies. She was learning the truth about wisdom. "The wise inherit honor, but fools he holds up to shame" Proverbs 3:35 (NIV).

Take time today to pursue the wisdom of God.

Did You Know ...

when Sophie needed wise answers, she pictured Jesus so she could talk to him better? Read *Sophie's Stormy Summer* to learn this technique.

More To Explore. Proverbs 2:10–12

GirL TaLk:

How much time do you spend in God's Word? How much effort do you make to regularly hear the wisdom of godly men, like your pastor?

God TaLk:

Lord, I need your wisdom in my life. Help me to pursue your wisdom with my whole heart. Amen.

BeauTy 101:

Seek wisdom. It can even make you look better! "How wonderful to be wise, to be able to analyze and interpret things. Wisdom lights up a person's face, softening its hardness" (Ecclesiastes 8:1 NLT).

Devotion #7

"Each of you should test your own actions."
—Galatians 6:4 (TNIV)

Can You Pass The Test?

Each person should be responsible for his or her own actions. Think about what you are doing. Do your actions show that you're a trustworthy person? Do you have high standards and work to the best of your ability? Take time to examine your actions.

Suppose you're having more and more trouble getting your homework done in the evenings. It shows up on your report card with a big dip in grades. "But it's not my fault!" you tell your parents. You share a room with your teenage sister, making it too noisy in your room to study. And you don't have Internet at home so you can't do research for your papers. And anyway, you just don't *get* geography. Even so, you know that your low grade isn't the best you could have done. Instead of laying blame elsewhere, examine your own actions.

You hate to admit it—even to yourself—but your study habits have slipped badly. You used to tackle your homework before supper, but now you spend that time on the phone. You used to study at the quiet kitchen table, but now you study on your bed, next to your sister's stereo and constantly ringing phone. You used to get your Internet research done in the school library, but lately during study hall you've passed notes and stared out the window. You have to admit it. After analyzing your own actions, you know the cause of your lower grades: your own behavior.

That's good news! When we test and examine our actions, we can usually find areas for improvement, places where a change could make a big difference. Take some time out now and examine your life, then make those positive changes.

Did You Know ...

it isn't up to other people to decide if you're doing your best? Instead, the Lord is the one who must decide. See 1 Corinthians 4:3–4.

Girl Talk:

What things in your life are you happy with? What would you like to do better? Examine and analyze your actions. Do you see areas for improvement?

More To Explore: 1 Corinthians 11:28

God Talk:

Lord, help me to do excellent work in everything I do. Instead of blaming others, help me to be responsible. Amen.

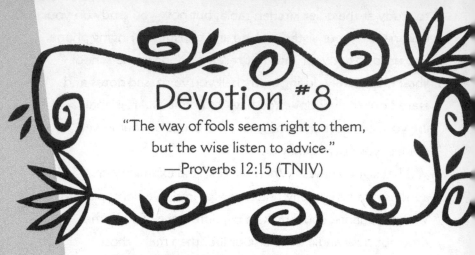

Devotion #8

"The way of fools seems right to them,
but the wise listen to advice."
—Proverbs 12:15 (TNIV)

Lend Me Your Ear

It's a foolish girl who thinks she never needs advice. Fools think that their opinions and actions are always right and that they know exactly what to say and do in every situation. A truly wise girl knows that she needs the advice of godly people.

At lunchtime Kylie was falsely accused by a teacher of leaving a pool of spilled milk on the floor. She hadn't done it, and she fumed as she cleaned up the mess. As she stewed, she mentally rehearsed what she intended to say to that lunchroom monitor. After all, she had to defend herself. She only planned to tell the truth. That teacher had no right to accuse her! When Kylie got through with her, that teacher would be begging for her forgiveness. Kylie's best friend tried to talk her out of having that heated confrontation, but Kylie wouldn't listen. After all, she was 100 percent right. What could be wrong with telling off that mean teacher? (As it turned out— *a lot*. Kylie ended up in detention for how she expressed herself.)

The Bible warns about the consequences we'll receive if we refuse to be guided by others' godly opinions. "Where there is no guidance the people fall, but in abundance of counselors there is victory" (Proverbs 11:14 NASB). Why is it so important to listen to others? Because we are so easily fooled into thinking we're doing the right thing. We can be very sincere in our beliefs—but still be sincerely wrong. "There is a way that appears to be right, but in the end it leads to death" (Proverbs 16:25 TNIV).

Be smart. Get advice from trusted people before making your decisions.

Did You Know ...

Jeremiah was once afraid that a king would kill him because he didn't like the advice Jeremiah gave him? See Jeremiah 38:15–28.

More To Explore: Proverbs 15:22

Girl Talk:

Do you have a problem you wish you could share with someone? Do you have a trusted adult to confide in: a teacher, pastor, counselor, parent, or grandparent?

God Talk:

Lord, sometimes I try to figure everything out by myself. It's scary to talk about my problems. Please give me courage to ask for advice. Amen.

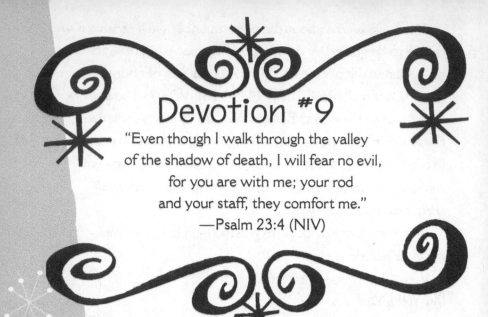

Devotion #9

"Even though I walk through the valley
of the shadow of death, I will fear no evil,
for you are with me; your rod
and your staff, they comfort me."
—Psalm 23:4 (NIV)

No Fear!

The rod and staff were sticks used by shepherds for counting, guiding, rescuing, and protecting their sheep. The Bible says that we are sheep, and Jesus is the Good Shepherd. Even if we are threatened with death, we don't need to be afraid. He is close beside us, to protect and comfort us.

We all need protection sometimes. You may not understand why girls at your middle school torment you. You're positive you've never said or done anything to them. Yet they taunt you about your weight, they make oinking noises when you pass them in the lunchroom, and they splash water on you in the restroom. They may not physically hurt you, but they terrify you just the same. The more you focus on what else they might do to you, the more scared you'll become.

What have you focused on recently? Is it God's Word, or is it a problem you're facing? If we focus on the fearful situation, it will appear impossible to overcome. Focusing on God's promises, on the other hand, gives us strength and lessens the fear. Start with these: "The LORD is with me; I will not be afraid. What can human beings do to me?" (Psalm 118:6 TNIV). "Though I walk in the midst of trouble, you pre-serve my life" (Psalm 138:7 NIV). "So do not fear, for I am with you; do not be dismayed, for I am your God. I will strengthen you and help you; I will uphold you with my righteous right hand" (Isaiah 41:10 NIV).

No matter what you're going through right now, your response can be, "I will *not* fear!" Speak it out loud forcefully several times. Focus on God's power, and you'll feel the comfort God promises.

Did You Know . . .

David was able to lie down and sleep peacefully, even when surrounded by thousands of his enemies, by trusting in God? See Psalm 3:5–6.

More To Explore: Psalms 27:1–3; 46:1–3

Girl Talk:

What things cause you fear? How do you feel when you focus on the problem? Do your feelings change when you concentrate on God's promises?

God Talk:

Lord, you haven't given me a spirit of fear. I trust you. Please help me to trust you even more. Amen.

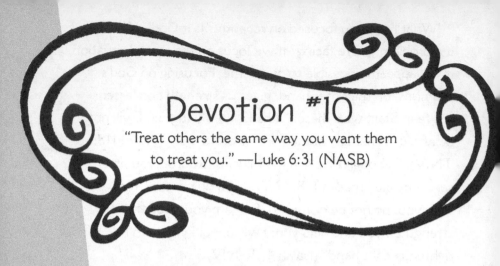

Devotion #10

"Treat others the same way you want them
to treat you." —Luke 6:31 (NASB)

For ALL The RighT Reasons

Jesus taught his followers to be considerate of others, to treat others with dignity and kindness. He said you should do for others the kinds of things you'd like them to do for you.

Emma had no trouble following this Golden Rule at school with her friends. She treated them with respect, she complimented them on their clothes, she helped with homework, and she cheered for them at volleyball games. But her home life was a different story. She snarled at her little brother when he accidentally bumped into her. She pronounced her sister's outfit dorky.

Jesus reminds us to treat others the way we want to be treated. Emma did that at school—but for the wrong reasons. She wasn't concerned about being loving or respectful. She just wanted certain girls to like her. At home, she didn't care what her brother and sister thought, and she treated them accordingly. Emma needs to examine her motives. We aren't supposed to love others in order to get something from them. "People may be pure in their own eyes, but the LORD examines their motives" (Proverbs 16:2 NLT).

Treat others the way you would like to be treated, but show love for the right reasons.

Did You Know ...

the Golden Rule is also called the "royal law"? See James 2:8.

More To Explore: Matthew 22:39

GirL TaLk:

In dealing with a friend, how does the Golden Rule help you know what to do? What about when people are nasty? How hard is it to love others then?

God TaLk:

Lord, I worry too much about how others treat me. Help me focus on how I treat others instead—and to treat them as I'd want to be treated. Amen.

Mini Quiz:

Yes or No. Did these girls follow the Golden Rule of Luke 6:31?
A. Ashley cheered Nicole up when she failed a test.
B. Amber refused to forgive her dad for missing her game.
C. Samantha spoke in a loving voice to her cranky sister.

(Answers: A. Yes [Ecclesiastes 4:10]; B. No [Luke 17:3-4]; C. Yes [Proverbs 17:17])

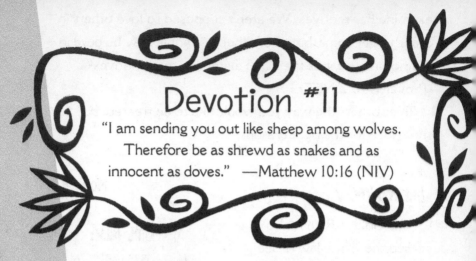

Devotion #11

"I am sending you out like sheep among wolves.
Therefore be as shrewd as snakes and as
innocent as doves." —Matthew 10:16 (NIV)

Be Prepared

Jesus warned his followers (and that includes you)
that the world was a dangerous place for them.
They were like sheep in the middle of a pack of
bloodthirsty wolves. Wolves hunted the sheep to kill
them. Jesus told his followers that if they wanted to survive living in this evil world, they needed to use their
sharpest, most clever intelligence, yet be gentle and without
sin. To live safely in our world today, Jesus' followers need to
do the very same things.

Maybe you tried out for cheerleading and won a spot on
the squad. Three of the cheerleaders returning from last
year have reputations for being cruel gossips. You're
determined to enjoy the cheerleading experience,
yet avoid being attacked by the backbiters. You
decide to stay alert and sharp. You even
make a game out of it, pretending you're
an undercover spy. The first moment
you detect gossip, you back away from
the group and won't participate. This
may irritate the gossipers, and they may

attack you with little digs, calling you a "goody-goody" and Miss Priss. If so, just laugh as if you believe they're innocently teasing you. Choose to be different from the group, no matter what it costs. Believers are to be "blameless and pure, children of God without fault in a crooked and depraved generation, in which you shine like stars in the universe" (Philippians 2:15 NIV).

Should you be afraid when out in the world? No, "because God has said, 'Never will I leave you; never will I forsake you.' So we say with confidence, 'The Lord is my helper; I will not be afraid. What can human beings do to me?'" (Hebrews 13:5–6 TNIV).

Did You Know ...

we need to be "shrewd as snakes" because the devil can transform himself into an appealing angel of light in order to fool us? See 2 Corinthians 11:14.

Girl Talk:

Are there places where you feel like a sheep among wolves? Is it at school, at home, or in your neighborhood? What can you do about it?

More To Explore: Ephesians 5:15

God Talk:

Lord, sometimes I don't even want to leave home. I feel out of place in the world, even attacked sometimes. Help me remember you are always with me, and for that reason I am safe. Amen.

Devotion #12

"Yet faith comes from listening to this message
of good news—the Good News about Christ."
—Romans 10:17 (NLT)

Walking by Faith

Having faith means having complete confidence in
God and his Word. It is believing—knowing deep
down—that something will happen, even before you see
proof. And this faith comes by listening to God's Word.

Dawn's faith was tested when her parents divorced, and
she moved from a small town to a big city. From a sprawling
house on a quiet street, she moved into a noisy fourth-floor
apartment. In her small school, she'd been in musical groups
and always had a part in the spring play. At her huge new
school, she felt like a drop of water in the ocean—
invisible and swallowed up. The life she'd always
planned was over. And yet, Dawn faced each
day expecting something good to happen.
She trusted that God had everything
under control and would bring good out
of it.

Where did she get such faith in the
face of so many unwelcome changes?

The Word of God. She repeated these verses every day: "'For know the plans I have for you,' declares the LORD, 'plans to prosper you and not to harm you, plans to give you hope and a future'" (Jeremiah 29:11 NIV); and "We know that in all things God works for the good of those who love him, who have been called according to his purpose" (Romans 8:28 NIV). Why does speaking God's Word have such power? "For the word of God is living and active. Sharper than any double-edged sword, it penetrates even to dividing soul and spirit, joints and marrow" (Hebrews 4:12 NIV). The Word of God is alive and powerful!

Faith isn't magic dust that someone sprinkles on you. It's very real and very solid. Build up your faith today. Get into the Word of God.

Did You Know ...

just hearing God's Word isn't enough? It needs to go down in the soil of your heart and take root. Read Luke 8:11–15 to see the four types of soil. Which kind are you?

More To Explore: Romans 1:16

Girl Talk:

What things do you have strong faith about? In what areas of your life is your faith weak?

God Talk:

Lord, thank you for your Word and its power to make my faith stronger. Help my faith in you to grow. Amen.

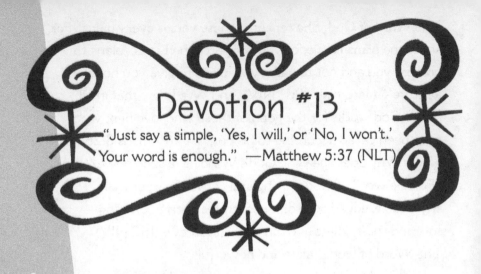

Devotion #13

"Just say a simple, 'Yes, I will,' or 'No, I won't.' Your word is enough." —Matthew 5:37 (NLT)

Just Say The Word

If someone asks you for a favor, make your decision and give a simple "Yes" or "No." You don't need to make lavish promises or give long-winded explanations. Your "Yes" or "No" is enough.

Suppose you tell your new friend a secret and make her promise not to tell anyone. Your friend promises. "I won't tell a living soul," she says. "I promise on a stack of Bibles. I *always* keep secrets. You can trust me. I've never broken a promise. Not ever!" By the time your friend is done, you have a funny feeling that she *would* blab your secret. You would have felt more reassured and trusting if your friend had merely said, "No, I won't tell." Even better, if you'd known your friend longer, you would know the girl's reputation. Only time can reveal whether someone can be trusted with secrets or if they will gossip about you. Only time can build trust in someone's character—you must see if what they *do* matches what they *say* they will do.

If a person is consistently truthful, she will develop a reputation for being honest. She won't need to make long promises. If she simply says, "Yes, I will," or "No, I won't," people will believe her. If a person is dishonest or a blabbermouth, getting her to promise won't mean much anyway. Dishonest people don't keep their promises at all well!

Strive to be honest and trustworthy in everything you do and with everyone you have contact. Then when someone asks you to do something, you can simply answer yes or no—and people will believe you.

Did You Know ...

many years ago, people didn't take oaths or sign many contracts or legal agreements? A man was "as good as his word" and "his word was his bond." In other words, his "yes" meant "yes." If he said he would do it, you could count on it. Is *your* word that reliable?

Girl Talk:

Which of your friends do you consider honest and trustworthy? Do they consider *you* the same?

More To Explore: James 5:12

God Talk:

Lord, I want to be honest in all that I say and do. Help me to be a girl people can trust. Amen.

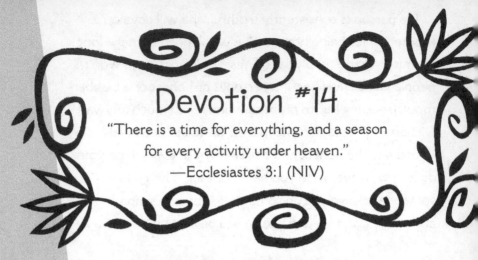

Devotion #14

"There is a time for everything, and a season
for every activity under heaven."
—Ecclesiastes 3:1 (NIV)

Growing and Changing

Things change. People change, families change,
bodies change, activities change—everything is
changing all the time. Sometimes we want to speed
up change, especially if we're waiting for something we
want. Sometimes our desire is to slow change or even
stop it, especially when something bad is happening. But
there is a right and proper time for everything.

Amber felt as if she were spinning dizzily on a merry-go-
round that whirled faster and faster—and she wanted to
jump off. New and unwelcome changes seemed to bombard
her every day. Her dad got a promotion, but it meant moving to another city. Lately her face was one big oil clog,
with new zits popping out hourly. Her older sister
had left for college, and while Amber enjoyed
her bigger bedroom, she missed having her
sister to confide in. Changes—if only
they'd stop! On the other hand, she
wished her body *would* change. She
hated being the only girl at her new
school who was still built like a boy.

If you're in the middle of changes—either wanted or unwanted—remember that things are *not* spinning out of control. God is the Master of all the times and seasons of your life. "Blessed be the name of God forever and ever, for wisdom and might are His. And He changes the times and the seasons" (Daniel 2:20–21 NKJV). God loves you, and you can trust him to bring about changes at exactly the right and proper time. Learn to say, "But as for me, I trust in You, O LORD; I say, 'You are my God.' My times are in Your hand" (Psalm 31:14–15 NKJV).

Yes, changes can be annoying, even scary. Learn to relax and let them happen naturally. There's a time for every purpose under heaven.

More To Explore: Ecclesiastes 3:17

Did You Know ...

there are even times and seasons for speaking certain words? See Proverbs 15:23.

Girl Talk:

What changes are you going through right now? Which changes do you wish were happening—but haven't yet?

God Talk:

Lord, I need to relax and stop fighting change. Help me to trust that you have everything under control. Amen.

Devotion #15

"Those who give heed to instruction prosper,
and blessed are those who trust in the LORD."
—Proverbs 16:20 (TNIV)

Getting a Life

Whoever closely follows the instructions in God's Word will prosper. To prosper means to get stronger, to gain wealth, and thrive. Happiness is found in trusting God's Word.

Suppose you share a locker at school with another girl. Your books and papers litter the bottom of the locker. One day the other girl yells at you. "Clean up this junk, you slob!" she snaps. You snarl back, "Get a life, girl. *Some* of us have more important things to do than clean lockers." She slams the locker door and says, "We'll see what Mrs. Sims says about this!" You stare, mouth open. Would this big baby really go to the principal about a messy locker?

That night, you report how your locker-mate yelled at you and how things got out of control. "Try a soothing voice next time," your mom says. "'A gentle answer turns away wrath, but harsh words stir up anger'" (Proverbs 15:1 NLT). You question your mom's advice, but it's worth a try. The next morning you're ready when the other girl snaps, "I told you to clean up this junk!" You take a deep breath and smile. "You're right. My stuff is a mess, and it's your locker too. I'll clean it up today during my study hall." Eyes wide, the other girl blinks and mumbles, "Good. Thanks," before heading down the hall.

God gives you instructions in his Word, but you must choose to either follow or refuse them. The decision is yours. God won't make the choice for you. In large part, the blessings in your life depend on your choices. "Whoever scorns instruction will pay for it, but whoever respects a command is rewarded" (Proverbs 13:13 TNIV).

Don't be stubborn and refuse instruction. Instead, treat it like your friend—because it is! Be smart, and be blessed!

Did You Know ...

because Joseph trusted God, God caused him to be taken from prison and promoted to a place of power in Egypt? Read Genesis 41:38–40.

God Talk:

I want my life to be successful and happy. Help me to follow your instructions closely. Amen.

More To Explore: Daniel 1:19–21

Girl Talk:

When have you been blessed by following good instructions? When have you suffered for ignoring wise advice?

Devotion #16

"She girds herself with strength and
makes her arms strong."
—Proverbs 31:17 (NASB)

Physical Fitness

A godly young woman prepares herself and builds
up her strength, making her arms strong. She is an
energetic and hard worker. The purpose of her physical fitness isn't for outward show, but in order to work
vigorously, with plenty of energy for her tasks.

Brittany didn't like the "baby fat" that rounded out her
stomach and gave her an extra chin. Constantly tired, she
picked up every cold and flu germ circulating at her school. She
decided to do something about it. Brittany followed a healthy
diet, eating plenty of fruits and vegetables and whole grains.
She jogged before school each morning. Slowly the fat
pounds melted off and were replaced by firm muscle.

Besides looking fit, Brittany was pleased to find she
could concentrate better at school, she slept
better at night, and after-school sports no
longer exhausted her. She performed her
many jobs more easily.

God has a plan for your life (see
Jeremiah 29:11), and if you're physically
fit you'll be able to follow that plan and

become all that God intended you to be. If you're a believer, there's another reason to keep your body fit: the Holy Spirit lives in you. "Or do you not know that your body is the temple of the Holy Spirit who is in you, whom you have from God, and you are not your own?" (1 Corinthians 6:19 NKJV). These are excellent reasons to be physically fit. However, don't let your motive for taking care of yourself be to impress others with your appearance. That's a dead-end street.

Why not start a fitness program today? It's true what is said about muscle: use it or lose it!

Did You Know ...

building strong muscles takes three things working together (exercise, healthy eating, and quality rest)?

God Talk:

Lord, I want to take good care of the body you've given me. Help me to eat right and exercise. Amen.

More To Explore: 1 Timothy 4:7–8

Girl Talk:

Do you take good care of your body? Do you eat healthy food and get enough exercise? Why do you want to be in good physical condition?

Beauty 101:

Running can cause "shin splints," a term for pain in the lower leg. The key to prevention is proper training. Be sure to warm up before, and stretch afterward.

Devotion #17

"To human beings belong the plans of the heart, but from the LORD comes the proper answer of the tongue."
—Proverbs 16:1 (TNIV)

Making Plans

We use our minds to think and plan and get organized. That's an important function of our minds. But if those plans are to work out, God must give us the ability to express those ideas and the strength to achieve those goals. Has this ever happened to you? You plot and plan how to convince your parents to increase your allowance and allow you to stay up later on weekends. You have all your arguments organized. You've even written them down. But when you start talking, you grow so frustrated at their questions that you can't remember any of your well-planned ideas. You blow up and run from the room. Later that night, you reread your list of convincing reasons, but take time to talk to God before talking to your parents. "Lord, please give me your words to say," you pray. "Make my words sound calm and sensible." Your second talk with your parents will go much better!

It's good to make plans and think about your goals, but always remember that God is still in control. He knows what's best and how plans will—or won't—work out. "In their hearts human beings plan their course, but the LORD establishes their steps" (Proverbs 16:9 TNIV). If you're a follower of Jesus, then it is up to him to lead the way. "LORD, I know that people's lives are not their own; it is not for them to direct their steps" (Jeremiah 10:23 TNIV).

Be organized. Make plans. Then give the plans to God to bring about.

Did You Know ...

God himself touched Jeremiah's mouth and told Jeremiah that he had put his very own words there? See Jeremiah 1:9.

More To Explore: Exodus 4:11–12

Girl Talk:

Are you organized with your homework, your jobs, and your spare time? Do you make plans? Do you depend on God's wisdom to carry them out?

God Talk:

Lord, I'm glad you're in control, even when I make all kinds of plans. Only you can make them work. Amen.

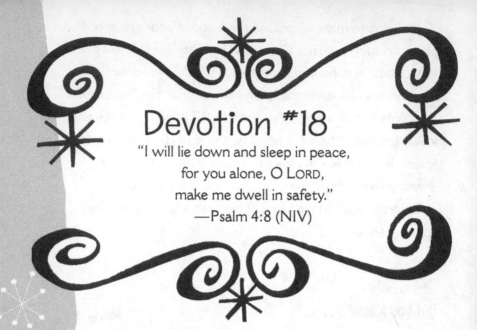

Devotion #18

"I will lie down and sleep in peace,
for you alone, O LORD,
make me dwell in safety."
—Psalm 4:8 (NIV)

Ahhh ... Sleep

You can go to sleep at night without mental stress or anxiety. God will take care of you. The Lord will guard you while you relax and rest.

Samantha never worried. She was too busy with school, cheerleading, babysitting, and her friends. But once she crawled into bed, fears invaded her mind. What would she do about the money she owed her best friend? When would she finish her history project? Why did her grandmother look so frail these days? Worries swirled around her mind, stealing her sleep.

Samantha was certainly *not* lying down and sleeping peacefully. She had temporarily forgotten that God is in command of everything. But she remembered one great secret: prayer will push out worry. So Samantha took each situation, one by one, and prayed for God's help and intervention. Step-by-step, she gave her worries to him, and at last she fell into a peaceful sleep. "Do not be anxious about anything, but in everything, by prayer and petition, with thanksgiving, present your requests to God. And the peace of God, which transcends all understanding, will guard your hearts and your minds in Christ Jesus" (Philippians 4:6–7 NIV).

Your safety and success don't depend on your worrying and planning. The Lord is your security. "You can lie down without fear and enjoy pleasant dreams. You need not be afraid of disaster or the destruction that comes upon the wicked, for the LORD is your security" (Proverbs 3:24–26 NLT). So tonight, pray and give God your worries. Then snuggle down and sleep, trusting him to take care of you.

Did You Know ...

caffeine (found in chocolate, and some sodas and teas) can cause a delay in falling asleep and can awaken you during the night?

More To Explore: Psalm 3:5

Girl Talk:

Do you ever worry yourself to sleep? Does that help solve your problems? What can you do instead?

God Talk:

Lord, please take care of me and all my concerns. Thank you for restful sleep. Amen.

Beauty 101:

Get your beauty sleep! Most kids and teens require at least nine hours of sleep per twenty-four-hour period. There's also a connection between sleep time and school performance—the shorter the sleep time at night, the lower the student's grade.

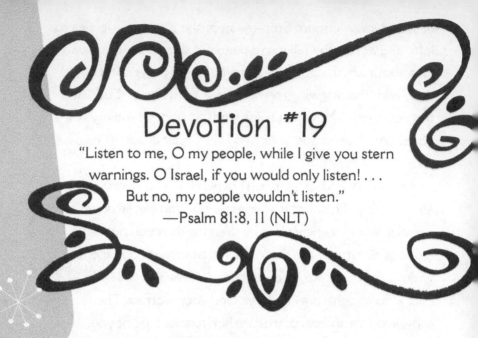

Devotion #19

"Listen to me, O my people, while I give you stern
warnings. O Israel, if you would only listen! . . .
But no, my people wouldn't listen."
—Psalm 81:8, 11 (NLT)

Are You Listening?

God wants his followers to listen to him. He gives
serious warnings to us when we are taking a wrong
path and headed in a bad direction. Like a frustrated parent, he too often sees his people refuse to listen to his
warnings.

You may have a talent for hearing only what you want to
hear. When you're on the phone with a friend, you can easily tune out your mother's call to help cook supper or
your dad's warning to finish your homework and get
to bed. Adults may be speaking to you, but no
one would know it by your responses.

Maybe you don't want to be disturbed, or
you just don't like what they're saying.
So you ignore them. Many times, we
ignore our heavenly Father the same
way.

We are told that the whole Bible is useful for straightening us out and teaching us to live our lives rightly (see 2 Timothy 3:16). Through the Bible, the Lord warns us of pitfalls and steers us in the right direction. God also sees our hard times and wants to comfort us. God is still speaking to us through his Word. Are you listening?

God's rules for living found in the Bible are given so we can live happy, healthy lives. So sharpen your hearing. Is God speaking to you? Pay attention and live!

Did You Know ...

God promised the Israelites that if they would obey his commandments, he would protect them from disease? See Exodus 15:26.

More To Explore: Isaiah 1:19–20

Girl Talk:

Do you listen to what God has to say in the Bible? If not, why not? If you do pay attention, what do you do with the instructions and warnings?

God Talk:

Lord, I need to listen to you better. Help me make the changes that need to be made in my life. Amen.

Fun Factoid:

Do your parents accuse you of being deaf? They could be partly right! The *decibel* is the unit used to measure loudness. Any sound above eighty-five decibels can cause hearing loss. (Noise from a lawnmower is ninety decibels.) Eight hours of such noise—which includes listening to music that is too loud—can cause damage to your hearing.

Devotion #20

"Who may ascend the mountain of the LORD?
Who may stand in his holy place?
Those who . . . do not put their trust in an idol."
—Psalm 24:3–4 (TNIV)

Me? Worship Idols?

There are certain standards you must meet before you approach God. If you want the Lord to hear your prayers, then you must not worship idols. God wants to be first in your life.

Morgan had heard about idol worship, but she knew that couldn't have anything to do with her. It was about bowing down to stone statues or worshiping things carved out of wood, wasn't it? Not necessarily. Morgan actually had an idol herself. His name was Chad. She thought about him day and night. She daydreamed about him instead of finishing her homework. She was too distracted to read, and too wound up to eat. When she dressed for school, she only wondered, *Will Chad like this outfit?* She thought about him first thing in the morning and last thing at night, plus plenty of time in between. Including during Sunday's sermon.

An idol doesn't have to be made of stone or wood or gold or look like a strange animal. An idol can be anyone who is adored blindly and excessively. When your feelings about another person totally absorb you, you've allowed that person to become an idol. When your intentions are to please him first and above all others, he's taken God's place in your life.

It's okay to like boys. It will happen more and more as you grow up. But it's *not* good or healthy to make a boy into an idol. The only person who belongs in first place in your life is the Lord.

Did You Know ...

in *Sophie's First Dance?*, Dr. Peter said the girls would know it was time to like boys when "being around them takes you closer to God, not further away." In other words, the time is right if you can like a boy without making him an idol that's more important than God.

GirL TaLk:

Who is the most important person to you? Does their opinion of you matter more to you than God's opinion?

More To Explore: Acts 14:11–15 and Exodus 20:3

God TaLk:

Lord, sometimes I put others ahead of you. Help me to keep you first in my life, no matter who else is important to me. Amen.

Devotion #21

"Wisdom will save you from the ways of wicked men, from men whose words are perverse."—Proverbs 2:12 (NIV)

Choosing Friends Wisely

Following God's instructions in the Bible will prevent you from making friends with people who are morally wrong and will hurt you. His guidelines for making friends will also keep you from liars whose words stir up trouble.

You and your neighbor may have been best friends since kindergarten, but lately something has changed. Your neighbor has begun lying to her parents about where she goes after school. She also seems to enjoy stirring up trouble in your group of friends by spreading rumors and making people mad at each other. "A troublemaker plants seeds of strife; gossip separates the best of friends" (Proverbs 16:28 NLT). These days you're also embarrassed by your friend's filthy language. The last straw comes when you get detention one day. Your friend breaks a rule at school, and because you happen to be with her, the teacher assumes you're guilty too. Your friend doesn't mind detention—in fact, she seems proud of it. You hate it, though.

You need to make a choice soon. Your reputation at school has been damaged, and your feelings have been hurt by the gossip. "Walk with the wise and become wise, for a companion of fools suffers harm" (Proverbs 13:20 TNIV). Frankly, you're tired of having her for a friend. She's changed too much. Even though your neighbor's been a good friend for years, she isn't the kind of friend God would choose for you now. She enjoys breaking rules and proclaims it to everyone. But "all who fear the LORD will hate evil. That is why I hate pride, arrogance, corruption, and perverted speech" (Proverbs 8:13 NLT). You can talk to your friend and explain your feelings, but it may only make her angry. If so, you may have to make a very difficult decision: not to hang with her anymore. Use wisdom and find friends whose values more closely match yours.

Did You Know ...

David (the psalm writer) also chose to avoid people who enjoyed doing evil and instead took a stand for the Lord? See Psalm 26:5–12.

More To Explore:

Proverbs 4:14–16 and 2 Corinthians 6:17

Girl Talk:

How do you choose your friends? To you, what are the qualities of a good friend?

God Talk:

Lord, I want to make wise choices about friends. Bring friends you choose into my life. Thank you for keeping me safe when I follow you. Amen.

Devotion #22

"But the LORD said to me, 'Tell them, "Do not go up
and fight, because I will not be with you.
You will be defeated by your enemies."'
So I told you, but you would not listen."
—Deuteronomy 1:42–43 (NIV)

Divine Defeat

The Lord told the Israelites to go into the Promised
Land and defeat those who lived there, but they refused.
They didn't believe God would protect them. So the Lord
told them to return to the wilderness. The Israelites changed
their minds, but God warned them it was too late. They dis-
obeyed and went to fight anyway—and were defeated. God
used defeat to get the attention of the stubborn Israelites.

Today God still gets our attention by allowing us to experience defeat.

Hannah's family was having problems, and the
tension made her edgy. She swallowed the
anxiety, but it erupted later as anger at her
best friend. She even mouthed off to her
reading teacher when she didn't have her
assignment done. Hannah was allowed
to experience defeat. Her best friend
refused to come over on the weekend.

She also spent time after school in the reading room. As she finished her overdue assignment, she prayed, "Lord, are you trying to tell me something?" That was the best prayer she could have prayed. It began the healing she needed. Later Hannah talked to a trusted adult friend about her fears and anger. Finding solutions—like apologizing for her behavior to her friend—got Hannah back on the success track.

Are things going badly in certain areas of your life? It may be that God is trying to get your attention to move you back on the path to joyful, peaceful living. Listen up!

Did You Know ...

the Israelites finally rebelled so often that they ran out of chances? God's patience ran out after they refused to obey so many times. More than six hundred thousand men (plus women and children) left Egypt, but none (except for Joshua and Caleb) were allowed to enter the Promised Land.

More To Explore: Isaiah 59:1-2

Girl Talk:

What are you having trouble with right now? Is anything going wrong in your life? Could God be trying to get your attention about something?

God Talk:

Lord, I want to take an honest look at my life and not blame my problems on others. Help me to listen to your words of wisdom. Amen.

Devotion #23

"When the LORD takes pleasure in anyone's way, he
causes their enemies to make peace with them."
—Proverbs 16:7 (TNIV)

Making Peace

Even when you have done nothing wrong, sometimes people won't like you. They may actually
hate you for no good reason! But if you try to do the
right things and treat others with kindness and respect
anyway, the Lord can make your enemies stop fighting
with you. In fact, they could end up liking you—and they
won't have a clue why!

Maybe you have never known why the older girls on your
bus torment you morning and night. They may tease you
about your clothes, your hair, your handicapped brother, and
your glasses. As far as you can remember, you've never
said or done anything bad to these girls. Even so, by the
time you arrive at school in the morning, you feel
battered, as if you've been through a war, even
though you haven't actually talked to them.
Still, you're polite when they block your
path and you have to step around them.
Their words knife through you,
though—and you want to insult them
back—but you refuse to be like them.

You pray and continue to do what you feel is right.

A month later you're shocked to receive a card in the mail, along with an apology from one of the girls for their treatment of you. While you continued to do what pleased God, he was working in the girls' hearts to bring peace to the situation.

What do you do while you're waiting for God to change your circumstances? Like the psalm writer, you run to the Lord. "For You have been a refuge for me, a tower of strength against the enemy. Let me dwell in Your tent forever; let me take refuge in the shelter of Your wings" (Psalm 61:3–4 NASB).

Did You Know . . .

God can make your enemies be at peace with you, even when those enemies are in your own family? See Genesis 33:1–4.

More To Explore Genesis 39:21–22

GirL TaLk:

Do you have any enemies? Are you being an enemy to someone else?

God TaLk:

Lord, I don't like having enemies. Help me to do what's right, no matter what. Amen.

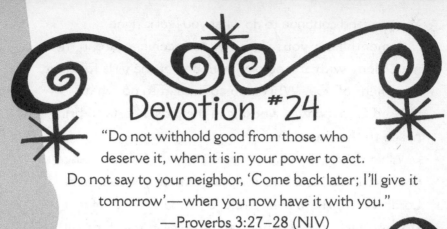

Devotion #24

"Do not withhold good from those who deserve it, when it is in your power to act. Do not say to your neighbor, 'Come back later; I'll give it tomorrow'—when you now have it with you."
—Proverbs 3:27–28 (NIV)

Be Generous

If you have something you could share with others, don't be stingy and hang on to it. Be generous with the poor. If they need something—and you have it—don't put them off with promises of help tomorrow. Help them today!

Rachel was awakened in the night by fire engines. Sirens screamed and lights flashed. Within an hour, a neighbor's house had burned to the ground. Everyone got out safely—a mother and four small children—but they lost everything. The next day her parents collected things for the family. Rachel was glad to help her mom pack up sheets and towels and canned goods for the neighbors. But when her mom suggested she add a few stuffed bears from her collection, Rachel paused. "Well, okay, I'll sort through them this weekend and decide which ones to give away." Her mom replied, "Those children have nothing left—no toys or clothes or beds. I think if they had teddy bears to hold tonight, it might help them." Rachel stared at the floor. "I hadn't thought of that. I'll get the bears now."

It's good to feel compassion for people, but that feeling needs to be followed by action. If you say you care, then show it by your behavior. "Suppose a brother or sister is without clothes and daily food. If one of you says to them, 'Go in peace; keep warm and well fed,' but does nothing about their physical needs, what good is it?" (James 2:15–16 TNIV). When you serve others, you'll be blessed with a special kind of happiness. Remember the words of Jesus: "It is more blessed to give than to receive" (Acts: 20:35 NIV).

Did You Know ...

rich people are told to share their wealth and become rich in good works as well as money? See 1 Timothy 6:17–19.

GirL TaLk:

Have you helped someone else by giving them something of yours? Who could use your help today?

More To ExpLore: Galatians 6:10

God TaLk:

Lord, I need to be more sensitive. Help me to notice people in need and then to help them generously. Amen.

Devotion #25

"So do not fear, for I am with you; do not be dismayed,
for I am your God. I will strengthen you and help you;
I will uphold you with my righteous right hand."
—Isaiah 41:10 (NIV)

Loneliness

God tells his followers not to be afraid because he is
with us. The everlasting God, who made the heavens and
the earth, is with *you*. God says to not be struck with fear or
dread, even though you sense danger. Don't anxiously look
about you at your circumstances. Instead, focus on God, who
will strengthen you in your time of need.

Suppose your parents divorce, and you have to move to a
new school district. The first day of school may be a lonely
experience. In fact, the whole first month you might
feel invisible. Your classmates already have best
friends to hang with. What if you never make
friends at the new school? You've never felt
so lonely. When you finally tell your
mom about it, she says, "I wish I could
go with you to school and be your best
friend, but I can't. However, I know
someone who *will* go with you." She

helps you understand that God will help you and give you strength and *never* leave you alone.

One way to fight loneliness (or any other problem) is to make the Bible verses personal to *you*. Say them out loud. You might say today's verse like this: "I do not fear, for God is with me; I am not dismayed, for he is my God. He will strengthen me and help me. He will hold me up with his righteous right hand." Making the verses personal and speaking them aloud will increase your trust in God. It can give you a peace and reassurance you never had before.

Even when you feel lonely, you're not alone. God is right there—holding tight to your hand as he holds you up.

Did You Know ...

the Lord spoke to Paul in a vision to let him know that he wasn't alone in the city of Corinth? See Acts 18:9–10.

More To Explore: Matthew 28:20 and John 14:27

Girl Talk:

Do you ever feel lonely, even in a group at school or with your family at home? Do you think Jesus ever felt lonely? What did he do about it?

God Talk:

Lord, sometimes I'm really lonely. Help me to remember to reach for your hand because you're always there. Amen.

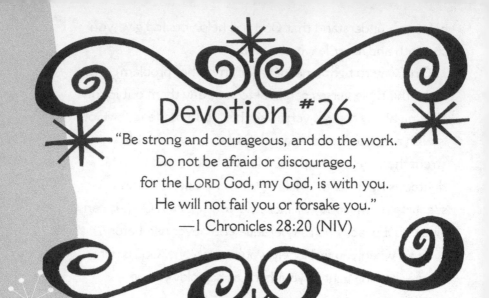

Devotion #26

"Be strong and courageous, and do the work.
Do not be afraid or discouraged,
for the LORD God, my God, is with you.
He will not fail you or forsake you."
—1 Chronicles 28:20 (NIV)

Press On with Courage

Sometimes the job God asks us to do looks enormous.
There's no earthly way we can do it. Yet we must be
strong and brave, not giving up, but pressing on to finish.
The size of a task—if stared at long enough—can cause fear
or discouragement to grip the heart. But if we remember that
God—the Creator of the whole universe—is with us, then
fear loses its power. God promises to work right there with
us—and he never fails.

Katie had prayed a long time before she took the job
as junior counselor at summer camp. But when she
arrived, she found she was in charge of six
homesick little girls. They cried, wouldn't
talk, and wanted to leave. Katie stepped
outside the cabin, gazed up at the stars
twinkling between the pine branches,
and prayed hard. She was scared at the
size of her job and discouraged by the

girls' behavior. However, a couple of minutes into her prayer, a peace settled over Katie's heart. She knew God was with her. He wouldn't fail her or leave her on her own. She just needed to "stand fast in the faith, be brave, be strong" (1 Corinthians 16:13 NKJV). She went back inside the cabin, got the lonely girls into sleeping bags, and chose this verse for their bedtime devotions: "Be strong in the Lord and in the power of His might" (Ephesians 6:10 NKJV).

No matter how big your task is, take heart. God won't leave you to handle it alone. He'll be right there beside you.

Did You Know ...

if you feed your faith, your fears will starve to death? Feed your faith by reading God's Word, praying, and thanking God for being with you and working things out. As your faith gets stronger, your fears will weaken.

More To Explore: Joshua 1:9

Girl Talk:

Are you facing a job or a challenge that seems too big for you? Do you need courage and strength from God to keep moving ahead?

God Talk:

Lord, help me remember that I'm never alone. Give me your courage to finish my work. Amen.

Devotion #27

"Let your eyes look straight ahead, fix your gaze
directly before you . . . Do not swerve to the right
or the left; keep your foot from evil."
—Proverbs 4:25, 27 (NIV)

Focus!

If you want to be successful in anything, you must
learn to focus. Keep your eyes trained on where you
want to go. Don't be looking to the right or the left. Look
straight ahead, and focus on the finish line.

Have you ridden a horse before? A horse can become skit-
tish and nervous when you ride him along country roads. He
swings his head from side to side, watches cars coming and
going, and jumps when he spots little animals scurrying in
the fields. After you put blinders on the horse, though, he
settles right down. With leather eye-patches sewn to
the sides of his bridle, a horse is prevented from
seeing things on either side. Distractions no
longer bother him. He faces forward, and
you both enjoy your rides much more.

Do you ever resemble such a horse?
Maybe you're learning to play the saxo-
phone. Or you're working and saving for
a bike. What happens when other inter-
esting things catch your attention? Do you

get sidetracked and forget your goal? Instead, keep moving forward toward your goal, and turn your eyes away from worthless things (see Psalm 119:37). Turning away from distracting things can be really hard to do! How do you find the strength to keep plugging along, especially when there isn't a reward for a long time? How can you stay steady and focused? You pray for help. Often. "Lead me, O LORD, in your righteousness because of my enemies—make straight your way before me" (Psalm 5:8 NIV).

Fix your eyes on whatever goal you have, and be determined to keep moving toward it in a straight line. Don't wander off the path and lose precious time. Stay focused! Concentrate. And reap the rewards in good time!

Did You Know ...

the Bible calls your eyes a lamp and says that if you focus on good things, you will be full of light? See Matthew 6:22.

Girl Talk:

Do you have trouble completing projects or tasks? Do you find yourself being distracted by other things? What can you do about it?

More To Explore: Joshua 1:7

God Talk:

Lord, I know I get scatterbrained sometimes. Help me to concentrate better. Keep me looking straight ahead. Amen.

Devotion #28

"The Spirit of the LORD will rest on him—the Spirit of wisdom and of understanding, the Spirit of counsel and of power, the Spirit of knowledge and of the fear of the LORD—and he will delight in the fear of the LORD. He will not judge by what he sees with his eyes, or decide by what he hears with his ears."

—Isaiah 11:2–3 (NIV)

Go With Your Gut

If you're a follower of Jesus, you have the Holy Spirit living inside you. He will give you understanding and knowledge of situations to guide you. You can't always make wise decisions based on what you see or hear.

Olivia was thrilled when Courtney invited her to her party. Olivia and her friends spent one whole afternoon deciding what they'd wear. When they heard Courtney was having a live band, they were even more excited. However, for no reason that Olivia could see, she started having funny, sick feelings in the pit of her stomach. She prayed about it, but the feeling only grew worse as the day of the party drew near. At the last minute, she decided to skip it. She stayed home alone that Saturday night, wondering if she'd made the right decision. On Monday—after hearing about the alcohol at the party and some property that had been destroyed—she silently thanked God for warning her to skip the party.

Colossians 3:15 (AMP) says to "let the peace (soul harmony which comes) from Christ rule (act as umpire continually) in your hearts [deciding and settling with finality all questions that arise in your minds]." If you don't have peace about a person, a situation, or an activity, pay attention! Then obey those "funny feelings" and avoid trouble. Don't let your friends convince you that you're imagining things. Trust the Holy Spirit's guidance, and let him keep you safe.

Did You Know ...

the Holy Spirit who lives in you is also called the Helper and the Spirit of truth? See John 15:26.

More To Explore: John 14:17

Girl Talk:

Can you think of some past times where you ended up in a bad situation? Before you went, did you have a "funny feeling" about that person or activity?

God Talk:

Lord, I need to listen to you when you try to warn me about things. Thank you for protecting me. Amen.

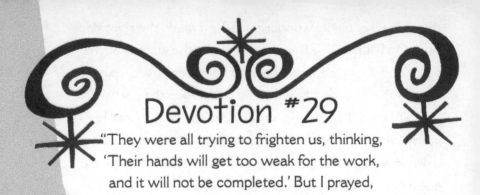

Devotion #29

"They were all trying to frighten us, thinking,
'Their hands will get too weak for the work,
and it will not be completed.' But I prayed,
'Now strengthen my hands.'"
—Nehemiah 6:9 (NIV)

Down in The Dumps

You may be surrounded by people who say, "You can't do that! You're weak! You'll never succeed!" If you listen to such voices, discouragement will set in. Don't pay any attention to them. Instead, pray. Ask God to give you strength to keep pressing on toward the finish line.

Maybe, for your science project, you decide to build a volcano that will really erupt. Every day in science class, two boys sitting beside you make jeering remarks. "What a stupid idea!" "That'll never work." "You'll never finish that ugly thing." You pretend not to notice, but at the end of each class, you're more unsure of your idea. When you tell your mom you want to change projects—and why—your mom prays with you about the hecklers. The next day you barely hear their comments—and your volcano is erupting by the end of the week.

Sometimes the people who discourage you are rivals. It might be the girl who warms the bench but wants your spot on the volleyball team. It might be the classmate who is competing with you for the lead in a school play. But sometimes those who make discouraging remarks are members of your own family—or a close friend. That's harder to bear. Once in a while, someone who loves you might try to discourage you because they're afraid you're trying something too difficult. No matter where a negative remark comes from, you don't have to accept it. Just say to yourself, *No, thank you! I'm not interested in any discouragement today!* and stay enthusiastic instead.

The next time you're working to achieve something, turn a deaf ear to people who try to discourage you. Instead, call on the Lord for *his* encouragement.

Did You Know . . .

real strength comes only from God? "But may the God of all grace . . . perfect, establish, strengthen, and settle you" (1 Peter 5:10–11 NKJV).

Girl Talk:

Do people make discouraging remarks to you? Do you make them to others—or do you try to encourage people?

More To Explore: Isaiah 35:3–4

God Talk:

Lord, I want to ignore people's negative remarks. Help me to listen only to you. Amen.

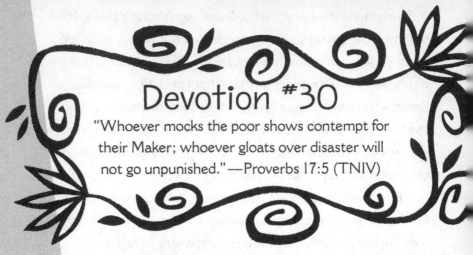

Devotion #30

"Whoever mocks the poor shows contempt for their Maker; whoever gloats over disaster will not go unpunished."—Proverbs 17:5 (TNIV)

No GLoaTing Zone

There are people who openly disrespect and make fun of the poor. This shows contempt for God, their Maker. If you're happy or smirk with satisfaction over people's disasters, you will be punished.

Heather was liked by many people, but a rich girl in her gym class constantly teased and tormented her. She ridiculed Heather's hand-me-down clothes, her pale skin, and her wild, frizzy hair. Then Heather heard that this girl's dad's business went broke, and they had to move from their fancy house to a small apartment. Heather laughed to herself and felt the girl deserved it. It was high time rotten stuff happened to that snob!

Heather secretly gloated to herself over this girl's disaster. She'd never admit it to anyone else, but she was delighted that Little Rich Girl was having serious trouble. God's Word says Heather will be punished for her attitude. That punishment can come in unexpected ways, either right away or in the future. What would have been a godly response instead? "Do not gloat when your enemies fall; when they stumble, do not let your heart rejoice" (Proverbs 24:17 TNIV). It's a choice to make, and Heather should have chosen *not* to be happy about it. Then she could have gone one step further. "Whoever oppresses the poor shows contempt for their Maker, but whoever is kind to the needy honors God" (Proverbs 14:31 TNIV). Heather could have offered a kind word to this girl about the situation. She might have prayed for her. Even in cases where people bring disaster on themselves, you can pray that they learn the lesson God wants to teach them.

When someone has trouble, treat them the way you'd want to be treated. You can't go wrong there.

Did You Know ...

if you have mercy on the poor, it will make *you* happy too? See Proverbs 14:21.

More To Explore: 1 John 3:17

Girl Talk:

Are you ever secretly glad when bad things happen to people you don't like?

God Talk:

Lord, I admit I've been happy when bad things happened to people who were mean to me. I don't want to be like that. Please change me. Amen.

Devotion #31

"For we are God's workmanship . . ."
—Ephesians 2:10 (NIV)

Work of Art

Each person is "God's workmanship." It means you're a masterpiece, a work of art! So learn to see yourself the way God sees you.

You may not feel like a work of art—no way! In fact, you may hate walking by mirrors, whether at home, at school, or when shopping. All you notice are your dorky glasses, or your zitty forehead, or your skinny figure. Although you are, in fact, an attractive young girl, you're so focused on the traits you dislike that you can't see anything else. You need to remember you're God's work of art. He created you just the way you are with a special plan in mind for your life.

Don't say negative things about yourself, like "I hate my nose" or "I'm too short" or "My stomach's fat." Don't downgrade yourself. Instead, say out loud every day, "I accept myself. God created me, and I'm his work of art. He has a wonderful future planned for me." Say this often enough, and you will gradually accept yourself as God's masterpiece. Why is this so important? If we

don't accept ourselves, we'll find it hard—if not impossible—
to accept others.

So smile. Really big. Remember—you're a work of art!

Did You Know ...

if you're a follower of Jesus,
you're also a completely *new*
work of art? See 2 Corinthians
5:17.

Girl Talk:

How do you feel about
your looks? Do you like
how God has made you?
Are there things you'd
like to change?

More To Explore: Psalm 100:3 and Isaiah 60:21

God Talk:

Lord, I want to accept myself
the way you made me. Help me to believe
that I am truly your masterpiece. Amen.

Mini Quiz:

Do you have a healthy body image? Answer "Yes" or
"No" to each question.

Q: Do you make up excuses not to dress for gym
class so no one will see you?

Q: When you admire a friend, do you mostly notice
her looks?

Q: Have you ever wanted to miss school because of
a zit or a bad haircut?

Q: Do you frequently criticize your body? (Example:
"My nose is too wide." "I wish my hair was a different
color." "Why are my feet so big?")

(The more "no" answers you gave, the better your self-
acceptance is.)

Devotion #32

"But if from there you seek the LORD your God, you will find him if you look for him with all your heart and with all your soul."
—Deuteronomy 4:29 (NIV)

Totally Involved

If you want to hear from God, you need to really search for him. You won't receive clear instructions if you give him little time or attention. A few minutes on Sunday or a couple of ten-second prayers during the week isn't enough. You must look for God with 100 percent of your heart and mind. He wants a full-custody relationship with you, not a weekend visit.

Cara's feelings about a boy in her neighborhood had her totally confused. Rumors said Troy was a little wild, and her parents didn't trust him after witnessing an angry explosion. Yet, he was funny, and he liked Cara. Just being near him made it hard for Cara to breathe. She wondered how God felt about her hanging with him. She prayed about Troy once in a while, but her feelings remained confused. Why didn't God answer her?

For one thing, Cara treated God like a vending machine. She tossed in her quarter (a minute of her time) and expected an answer to fall into her hand. She wasn't seeking God with her whole heart and mind. One day, after fighting with her mom about Troy, Cara shut herself in her room and got serious. She opened her Bible, prayed, read, and prayed some more. Certain verses stuck out, such as "Keep away from angry, short-tempered people, or you will learn to be like them and endanger your soul" (Proverbs 22:24–25 NLT). Lying on her bed, she waited and listened. By the end of the morning, she had her answer. It wasn't what she'd hoped for, but she felt God was impressing on her to avoid Troy.

God is there for you at all times. Seek him with your whole heart and an open mind, and you *will* find him.

Did You Know ...

the Lord promised to rescue the Israelite people from seventy years of slavery in Babylon after they chose to seek him with their whole hearts? See Jeremiah 29:10–14.

More To Explore: 2 Chronicles 31:21

Girl Talk:

How is your relationship with God? Is he like a casual acquaintance? A good friend? A loving father? How much time do you spend with him?

God Talk:

Lord, sometimes I rush through my time with you. Show me how to seek you with my whole heart. Amen.

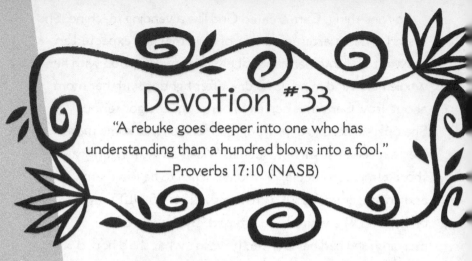

Devotion #33

"A rebuke goes deeper into one who has
understanding than a hundred blows into a fool."
—Proverbs 17:10 (NASB)

Caught in the Act

Sometimes people do wrong things and need to be corrected. A wise person with good sense will need a lecture or a scolding only in order to learn from her mistake. The Bible says a fool (one who lacks good judgment) won't learn much even from a beating.

Suppose you've agreed to see a movie with your friend on Friday night, and she's looking forward to it. Then, on Wednesday, a popular girl in your class invites you to a party—also for Friday night. Do you barely give it a thought and happily accept the invitation? You could call your friend and tell her you have to babysit on Friday, but that you can go to the movie on Saturday instead. It works! Then, when you hang up and turn around, your dad is standing there. From his disapproving look, you realize that he's heard the whole thing.

"Come with me," he says quietly, leading the way to the family room.

For a few minutes he talks about honesty and what it means to be a loyal friend. Keeping your word, he says, is one way to be loyal. He was disappointed to hear you lie to your friend. He doesn't tell you what to do. Instead, he leaves the decision up to you. Up in your room, you sink onto your bed. You know your dad is right. You truly want to be a person who can be counted on to keep her word. You make the wise decision and come clean with your friend. "Only a fool despises a parent's discipline; whoever learns from correction is wise" (Proverbs 15:5 NLT).

Don't be a person who has to be corrected severely before learning from her mistakes. Be wise instead. "Instruct the wise and they will be wiser still; teach the righteous and they will add to their learning" (Proverbs 9:9 TNIV).

Did You Know ...

David (the psalmist) called punishment a kindness and correction excellent oil? See Psalm 141:5 NKJV.

Girl Talk:

How do you respond when a parent or a teacher corrects you? Are you a wise girl or a foolish one?

More To Explore: Proverbs 13:1

God Talk:

Lord, I know I need correction sometimes. Help me to listen to it with an open mind and heart. Amen.

Devotion #34

"Those of us who are strong and able in the
faith need to step in and lend a hand to those
who falter, and not just do what is most convenient
for us. Strength is for service, not status."
—Romans 15:1 (MSG)

Lend a Hand

There are things we may feel are perfectly fine to do,
but that other followers of Jesus don't agree with.
Christians should not insist on doing what they want
without considering the feelings and strong beliefs of other
Christians. We may know that certain things make no difference, but we must be considerate of the doubts and
fears of those who think these things are wrong.

Jamie and her new friend went to the mall to shop.
Jamie spotted a G-rated movie at the theater complex
that she wanted to see. "Let's call home and ask if
we can stay for the movie," she said. Her
friend frowned, then said, "I don't go to
movies. My church teaches that movies
are wrong." Surprised, Jamie wanted to
argue and make her change her mind.
Jamie's own parents were strict about
what movies she was allowed to see, and

she knew her dad had already thoroughly checked this new movie out. Instead, she smiled and said, "No problem. Want to come home with me and make some chocolate chip cookies instead?"

Jamie was sure in her own heart that there was nothing wrong with the movie, but her new friend didn't feel the freedom to go. Jamie was considerate in not arguing and pushing to get her own way. As 1 Thessalonians 5:14 (NLT) says, "Encourage those who are timid. Take tender care of those who are weak. Be patient with everyone." Be willing to serve others and not always insist on your own way.

Did You Know ...

the Old Testament even has laws and rules about helping weak animals, like donkeys and oxen? See Deuteronomy 22:4.

More To Explore: Galatians 6:2

Girl Talk:

Have you given in to someone's wishes this week, either at home or at school? How often do you insist on having your own way instead?

God Talk:

Lord, help me to think of others more than myself. I want to encourage others the way you encourage me. Amen.

Devotion #35

"Plans fail for lack of counsel, but with many advisers they succeed." —Proverbs 15:22 (NIV)

Seek Advice

It's good to carefully plan projects, but those plans often don't work out if you fail to ask advice during the planning stage. If you listen to many advisers, your projects are more likely to succeed.

Suppose you and your best friend are tired of having no privacy from your younger brothers and sisters. You decide to build a tree house where you can be left alone. Your dad offers to help with the tree house plans, but you say you don't need help. He gives you a book on building projects, but you don't bother to open it. You and your friend already know exactly the kind of tree house you want. You work till sundown two nights in a row to build your creation. The following night you plan to camp out in the tree house. Unfortunately, you've built the little house on a dying branch. The limb breaks during the night, and in the morning you find the tree house on the ground, smashed to pieces. Before you rebuild, you decide to consult your dad and study his building book.

Pride and being overconfident can keep us from asking for advice. That's usually a mistake! No one is smart enough to do everything on her own. The right counsel can make the difference between success and failure, between victory and defeat. "The way of fools seems right to them, but the wise listen to advice" Proverbs 12:15 (TNIV). *One caution!* Be sure, when you ask advice, to compare that advice to biblical principles. (For example, if you need ten dollars, and your friend says to swipe it from your mom's purse, recognize that it's stealing. Ignore that advice!)

Listen to wise people, learn from their experience, and succeed!

Did You Know ...

when King Hezekiah discovered that the kings of Assyria had come to make war against Jerusalem, he asked the advice of his leaders and commanders on how they could stop the invasion? See 2 Chronicles 32:2–4.

Girl Talk:

When you have a problem, do you ask for advice? How do you choose the best people to ask? Do you then listen to their advice?

More To Explore: Proverbs 19:20

God Talk:

Lord, thank you for giving me people who care about me. Help me to listen to wise advice. Amen.

Devotion #36

"The beginning of strife is as when water first
trickles [from a crack in a dam]; therefore
stop contention before it becomes
worse and quarreling breaks out."
—Proverbs 17:14 (AMP)

Don't Burst The Dam!

Have you ever seen a dam in a river or a lake? Usually
made from cement, a dam holds the water back. But a tiny
crack in the dam, if left unrepaired, can get bigger fast. If the
dam breaks, the backed-up water can destroy homes and
crops. The beginning of a fight is like the crack in the dam. If
you deal with the disagreement immediately, it's easily fixed.
If not, quarreling quickly breaks out.

Rebecca had the same fight with her mom every Saturday morning. Rebecca thought her room looked
comfortable. Even cool. Her mom called it a pig-
pen. On her way out the door to her job,
Rebecca's mom always stopped by her
room and said, "Young lady, when I get
home today, this room had better be
spotless." Rebecca always demanded,
"What's wrong with it?" Her mom
yelled, "Dirty clothes on the floor. Empty

soda cans. Moldy food. Get this mess clean, or you're grounded!" Rebecca's shouts of "That's not fair!" followed her mom as she left for work.

A person who quarrels invites many problems into her life (see Proverbs 17:19). Next Saturday, what could Rebecca do differently? Instead of snarling, "What's wrong with my room?" Rebecca could simply say, "Okay, I'll clean it." Simple. Easy. Stops the leak in the dam immediately. No quarrel.

Some people insist on having the last word in a disagreement. Actually, a person who can bite her tongue and be silent in order to stop a fight is highly respected. "It is to one's honor to avoid strife, but every fool is quick to quarrel" (Proverbs 20:3 TNIV).

Did You Know ...

if you have wisdom from God, your actions will be characterized as being peaceable and willing to yield to others? See James 3:17.

GirL TaLk:

What kinds of quarrels do you get pulled into? What can you do to end them?

More To Explore: Proverbs 26:21

God TaLk:

Lord, I want to end fights before they start. Please show me how. Amen.

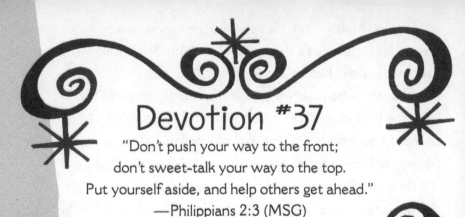

Devotion #37

"Don't push your way to the front;
don't sweet-talk your way to the top.
Put yourself aside, and help others get ahead."
—Philippians 2:3 (MSG)

Pushy, Pushy

We're all born with a leaning toward selfishness.
Secretly we'd all love to be first in everything. It's not
wrong to want awards and approval, but don't live to make
a good impression on others. We shouldn't push ourselves
to the front. Followers of Jesus help *others* into those top
positions.

You might know that your sewing teacher will soon
choose a girl to act as emcee for the class' fashion show.
You don't want to just model the outfit you sewed in
class. Instead, you want to introduce everyone
and be onstage the whole time. That way you
could show your parents that in school (at
least) you're valued. For several days,
you're extra sweet and helpful and com-
plimentary to your teacher. However,
on Friday your best friend, Caitlyn, says,
"Knock off all the buttering-up. Everyone

knows what you're doing. Stop acting so hot." You blush. Were you that obvious? You admit that Caitlin has just as much right to be the announcer. You also know that Romans 12:10 (TNIV) says, "Be devoted to one another in love. Honor one another above yourselves." So on Monday, when you talk to your teacher, you casually mention that Caitlin would be the perfect emcee for the fashion show.

Instead of pushing your way to the top, give others a boost instead. You can be sure of this: if the Lord wants you in the spotlight, he will make sure others notice you and promote you. "Humble yourselves in the sight of the Lord, and He will lift you up" (James 4:10 NKJV).

Did You Know ...

the apostle Paul felt that he was the lowest of all the apostles and, in fact, not even worthy to be called an apostle? See 1 Corinthians 15:9.

More To Explore: Proverbs 11:2; 13:10

Girl Talk:

Do you have a problem with pride? Are there areas where you think too highly of yourself?

God Talk:

Lord, I think too much about my own selfish interests. Help me to focus more on others' needs. Amen.

Mini Quiz:

True or False? Proud people

A. put down godly people.

B. help the poor.

C. help keep the peace.

D. should not be admired.

(Answers: A. True [Psalm 119:51]; B. False [Psalm 40:4]); C. False [Proverbs 28:25]; D. True [Psalm 10:2];

Devotion #38

"I am God, and there is no other; I am God,
and there is none like me . . .
What I have said, that will I bring about;
what I have planned, that will I do."
—Isaiah 46:9, 11 (NIV)

Do You Promise?

God is totally trustworthy. If he says he will do something,
you can count on it getting done. He isn't like a human
being. He always tells the truth, and whatever he promises
to do, he *will* do!

Believers should imitate God and also be trustworthy.
Brianna thought of herself as dependable and honest, but
was she really? Let's see. If her best friend asked how she
liked her new miniskirt, Brianna said she loved it. (She
secretly thought it was much too tight and short for
her friend's chunky figure.) If she had a babysitting job, but a friend asked her to a
movie, she called the family and said
she'd forgotten about some previous
plans. Then she went to the movie. If
her dad asked where she went after
school, Brianna said she stopped at the

library. (She did stop there, but only to drop off some overdue books before heading to the mall.) Was Brianna truly honest and dependable? Or was she just fooling herself?

God is 100 percent honest. He never deceives, and he can be depended on. "God is not a human, that he should lie, not a human being, that he should change his mind. Does he speak and then not act? Does he promise and not fulfill?" (Numbers 23:19 TNIV). If we are followers of Jesus, we must strive to be honest and dependable at all times too.

Did You Know ...

George Washington probably didn't chop down a cherry tree, but he did have a reputation for honesty? He said, "I hope I shall always possess firmness and virtue enough to maintain what I consider the most enviable of all titles, the character of an honest man."

More To Explore: Isaiah 45:5–5

Girl Talk:

Are you always honest? Can you be honest with your friends without being cruel or hurting their feelings? Is it ever right to tell a "white lie"?

God Talk:

Lord, I want to be a girl my friends and family can count on. Help me to keep my word, no matter how hard it is sometimes. Amen.

Devotion #39

"Turn from your sins and turn to God,
because the Kingdom of Heaven is near . . .
Prove by the way you live that you have really
turned from your sins and turned to God."
—Matthew 3:2, 8 (NLT)

Talk Is Cheap

John the Baptist was preaching about repentance. Repenting is not only changing your mind—it's a total turnaround of your life. It involves turning *from* sin and turning *to* God. It's not enough to say, "I'm sorry for my sins." Prove you're truly sorry by the way you live.

You may find a young brother or sister very annoying. He hogs the TV after school. She wolfs down all the good snacks, and then eavesdrops on your phone calls. Usually, before the night is over, you've swatted a sibling at least once. Your brother or sister runs screaming to your mom, who in turn scolds you. "I'm sorry," you always mumble. Sometimes you truly *are* sorry. One night, though, your mom says, "I don't want another apology, honey. Talk is cheap. If you're sorry, then show it. Stop hitting."

You need to do more than say you're sorry. No one will believe you forever. If you really regret your behavior, you'll change. However, repentance doesn't start with altering one's behavior. For change to last, it must begin with a change of heart. Let the Holy Spirit control you. Then "the fruit of the Spirit is love, joy, peace, patience, kindness, goodness, faithfulness, gentleness and self-control" (Galatians 5:22–23 NIV).

Don't just give lip service to repenting. Don't be that kind of friend. In addition, don't keep a friend who hurts *you* repeatedly, then apologizes, but keeps doing the same thing. True repentance is backed up by action. And what is the reaction in heaven when a sinner repents? "I say to you that likewise there will be more joy in heaven over one sinner who repents than over ninety-nine just persons who need no repentance" (Luke 15:7 NKJV).

Did You Know ...

Jesus rebuked the cities where he had done mighty miracles and yet the people refused to repent? See Matthew 11:20–24.

More To Explore

Ezekiel 18:30–32; 33:1

Girl Talk:

Do you apologize so someone will stop being mad at you? Or do you truly intend to change your behavior?

God Talk:

Lord, I can't change myself. I've already tried! Please change me from the inside out. Amen.

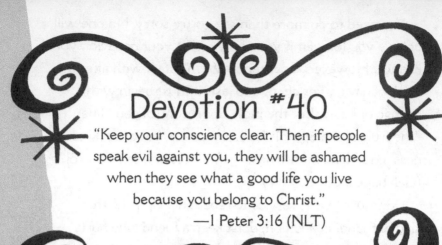

Devotion #40

"Keep your conscience clear. Then if people speak evil against you, they will be ashamed when they see what a good life you live because you belong to Christ."
—1 Peter 3:16 (NLT)

False Accusations

Be honest and do what is right. Pay close attention to your sense of right and wrong. Then if someone unfairly blames you for something, people won't believe the lies. The accusations will be shown to be untrue because of the way you live your life.

During volleyball practice, Alexis went to the locker room to use the restroom and then returned to the gym. Later, two girls discovered that money and phone cards were stolen from their clothes. Alexis explained that she didn't steal anything, and she didn't see anyone in the locker room when she walked through. Even so, the coach called her in the next day and accused her of the thefts. Alexis was stunned. She couldn't prove she was innocent, and she felt sick to her stomach by the time she was allowed to leave.

Alexis didn't know what else to do, so she simply kept living her life in the same way she always had. She did what was right and honest. She was grateful that she already had a reputation among her classmates for being trustworthy. Because of that, she found that few—if any—people believed the false accusations. "Be careful how you live among your unbelieving neighbors. Even if they accuse you of doing wrong, they will see your honorable behavior, and they will believe and give honor to God when he comes to judge the world" (1 Peter 2:12 NLT).

How believers respond to false accusations made against them shows the unbelieving world an important lesson. Live your life in such an honest way that no one will believe any lies told about you.

Did You Know ...

Paul relied on the Holy Spirit and his conscience to know if he was doing something wrong? See Romans 9:1 and 2 Corinthians 1:12.

God Talk:

Lord, I hate when people tell lies about me. It hurts. Help me to forgive those who accuse me. Please reveal the truth to them. Amen.

More To Explore:
Hebrews 13:18

Girl Talk:

Have you ever been falsely accused of something? How did it make you feel? Have you ever wrongly accused someone else? If so, take time to apologize.

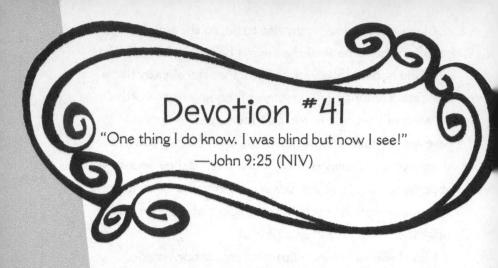

Devotion #41

"One thing I do know. I was blind but now I see!"
—John 9:25 (NIV)

Can't Argue With That!

When Jesus healed the blind man, the religious leaders refused to believe the man. They claimed Jesus was a sinner and had no power to perform miracles. The formerly blind man said he knew only one thing: he'd been blind, but since Jesus touched him, he could see! He gladly told others how Jesus had healed him.

You may have heard for years in Sunday school class that you should share Jesus with your unsaved friends. You want to, but for some reason you just can't. You may not feel smart enough. Maybe you haven't memorized enough verses to prove your points. Or you get tongue-tied easily. But one day in the restroom, you find a girl sobbing her heart out. You discover that this girl's dad has left his family. Your own dad died two years before in a car accident. Without thinking or being nervous, you simply talk to the hurting girl. You tell her how Jesus was your best friend when your dad died. You'd been so terrified and lonely, and Jesus filled that empty place in your heart. Simply describing what your life was like before—and after—knowing Jesus can comfort someone's wounded heart.

The healed blind man did the same thing. No matter how the Pharisees argued, they couldn't debate one basic fact: *the blind man could now see*. That was his testimony. The same is true today. People simply can't argue against the truth of your experience with Jesus.

More To Explore: Luke 7:21-22

Did You Know ...

there is also spiritual blindness, and Jesus even called the Pharisees "the blind leading the blind"? See Matthew 15:14.

GirL TaLk:

Have you ever shared about Jesus with an unsaved friend or family member? How did that go?

God TaLk:

Lord, thank you for being the best friend I ever had. Help me to be bold in telling others about you. They need you too. Amen.

BeauTy 101:

Don't become a blind girl! You can be blinded by the sun. Sunglasses should be worn daily, especially between 10:00 a.m. and 2:00 p.m., when ultraviolet exposure is the most dangerous. Effective sunglasses should block both UVA and UVB radiation. Ordinary sunglasses make the situation worse! The dark lenses cause the pupils to dilate, allowing more of the dangerous UVA radiation to damage the lens and retina.

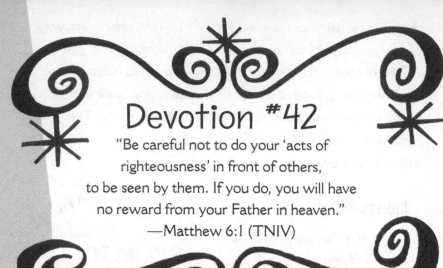

Devotion #42

"Be careful not to do your 'acts of
righteousness' in front of others,
to be seen by them. If you do, you will have
no reward from your Father in heaven."
—Matthew 6:1 (TNIV)

Showing Off

It's good to help the poor and do other good deeds, but why are you doing them? Is it to be admired and call attention to your giving? That's a poor attitude. Do your good deeds quietly instead. Let your reward come from God in heaven.

Ashley's sixth-grade class decided to do something to help victims of three tornadoes that had swept across her state. They each collected blankets, clothing, and canned foods in their own neighborhoods. The donated items were to be taken to a drop-off site, where they'd be loaded in a big truck and transported to the victims. While Ashley's dad drove her to the drop-off site, she was tired, but she was glad she'd spent the day getting donations. The next night, the local newspaper carried a front-page story about the sixth-grade's volunteer work. Ashley's lip curled at the large photo by the article. It was a close-up of Danielle, a girl in her class. Her dad owned the newspaper. The photo showed many things Danielle's family had personally donated to the relief efforts. In the article, they were praised so much it sounded like they'd organized the whole thing.

When you give, think about your reasons. Are you doing it because you truly care? Or are you, like Danielle's family, wanting others to see what you're doing and praise you for it? God knows your reasons, and he knows the secrets of your heart (see Psalm 44:21). Do help others, but don't call attention to yourself in the process, showing off how "good" you are. "But when you give to someone . . . give your gifts in secret, and your Father, who knows all secrets, will reward you" (Matthew 6:3–4 NLT). Remember how blessed you are. Be willing, from your heart, to help others.

Did You Know ...

Jesus told a story about a man who quietly did a very good deed for someone who'd been beaten and robbed? (See Luke 10:30–35.)

Girl Talk:

Why do you help others? Do you secretly hope others will notice?

More To Explore: Matthew 6:6

≦God Talk:

Lord, I want to give for pure reasons. Help me to care about only *your* opinion. Amen.

Devotion #43

"Do not judge, and you will not be judged.
Do not condemn, and you will not be condemned
Forgive, and you will be forgiven."—Luke 6:37 (NIV)

CUTTing DoWn

No one enjoys being around someone who is a faultfinder. Don't be a girl who puts others under a microscope, searching for flaws and defects to point out to others. If you judge others, expect the same thing to happen to you. It might not happen immediately—and the judging might be behind your back—but it *will* happen. Why not go easy on others instead? Then they will do the same for you.

Maybe you think the girl who sits next to you in band smells odd, and she squeaks like a hyperactive mouse. After band, your best friend pinches her nose and points to Miss Mouse as she leaves. What should you do? Join in and make fun of her? Share the weird things Mouse did during the hour? It's tempting, even though James 4:11 (NKJV) says, "Do not speak evil of one another." Why do we like to do it then? Usually to feel better about ourselves. Cutting someone down makes us feel more important, but it's an unloving thing to do. Don't do it, no matter how tempting.

We tend to put other people's faults under a microscope and make the faults even bigger. But we make excuses for our own faults. Instead, examine your *own* behavior and learn to accept others, warts and all. Then you'll be in the happy position of having others do that for you.

Did You Know ...

Jesus said judgmental people try to pick a speck of dust out of someone else's eye while they have *logs* sticking out of their own eyes? See Matthew 7:3–4.

More To Explore: Romans 2:1

Girl Talk:

Have you judged or criticized anyone at school or in your family? Has someone judged or criticized you? How did it make you feel?

God Talk:

Lord, I don't want to be a faultfinder. Please help me talk about others the way I want them to talk about me. Amen.

Beauty 101:

Watch your face in the mirror as you say something critical and judgmental about someone. Then watch your face change when you say something warm and kind about someone. Which is more beautiful to look at, the frowning, judgmental sneer—or the smile of kindness?

Devotion #44

"Don't copy the behavior and customs of this world,
but let God transform you into a new person by
changing the way you think. Then you will know
what God wants you to do, and you will know how
good and pleasing and perfect his will really is."
—Romans 12:2 (NLT)

Brand-New

The world is full of evil practices, violence, and dishonesty.
Don't copy the ways of the world! Instead, let God change
you from the inside out into a new person by changing your
thinking. This changing—or transforming—isn't a one-time
event. It's a process that takes time, much like the process of
a caterpillar changing into a butterfly. After the transformation has taken place, you—like the butterfly—will see the
wonderful plan God has for your life.

Jenna was miserable. She'd accepted Jesus as
her Savior at church camp the summer
before. But no one at school knew it. She
still hung out with the same kids, talked
the same way, watched the same
movies, and dressed the same. Only
now she felt wrong, out of place, and

guilty. She knew she didn't belong in those places anymore. Finally, in desperation, she stayed home one weekend, pretending to be sick. She read and thought about huge chunks of her Bible: John, Psalms, and Proverbs. By the end of the weekend, she decided to stop copying the behavior of the world.

God wants you to have a joyful, abundant life, but you need to grow up as a Christian. God gave you a new spirit, not a new brain. Your mind still has its old sinful patterns. It needs to be transformed by reading God's Word and thinking how to apply it in your everyday life. In time, you'll experience "love, joy, peace, patience, kindness, goodness, faithfulness, gentleness and self-control" (Galatians 5:22–23 NIV).

Did You Know ...

if you help the butterfly break out of his cocoon, his wings will be too weak to fly? The butterfly needs the struggle to strengthen his wings. All transformation involves struggle—but it's worth it.

More To Explore: 1 John 2:15

Girl Talk:

Are there areas of your mind that need changing? What can you do to start the process?

God Talk:

Lord, I want to be more like you. Show me what my part is—and help me to do it. Amen.

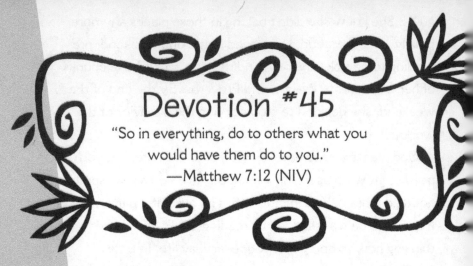

Devotion #45

"So in everything, do to others what you
would have them do to you."
—Matthew 7:12 (NIV)

GoLden RuLe

Decide how you would like to be treated. Then in everything you say and do, treat others that way first.

For example, what if you overhear your parents fighting after you go to bed at night? Several of your friends have divorced parents, and you're terrified of this happening in your family. One Saturday morning, when your mom is eating breakfast, you sit down beside her and ask, "Mom? I need to know something. What's wrong between you and Dad? I hear you fighting at night." Your mom presses her lips together. "You must be hearing the TV. Your dad and I don't fight. There's nothing for you to worry about."

For a long time you sit in silence. You want and need your mom to be honest with you. Maybe you need to be totally honest first. "Mom, it's not the TV. And I do worry. I don't want you getting a divorce. Are you?" Your mom sets her coffee mug down, stares at you for a minute, then says, "You're right. We've been fighting. We're not getting a divorce, but we do need help with our problems. We're going to counseling this week."

If you're direct with people, you're more likely to receive honesty in return. This "Golden Rule" can show you how to act in most situations. How should you treat the new girl in class? Well, how would you like to be treated if you were new? Would you like someone to show you around the building and sit by you at lunch? Then do those things for the new girl. If you fight with someone, how do you want to be treated? Do you want her to listen to you explain without being interrupted? Do you want her to apologize for her part in the fight? Then do likewise when someone is mad at *you*. "Love other people as well as you do yourself" (Romans 13:9 MSG).

Did You Know ...

there are websites about the Golden Rule and even books on running a business using this idea?

More To Explore: Galatians 5:13–15

Girl Talk:

Are you willing to *first* treat others the way you want to be treated? Is it hard to do?

God Talk:

Lord, help me to put myself in someone else's shoes and then treat them the way I want to be treated. Amen.

Devotion #46

"You do not have, because you do not ask God."
—James 4:2 (NIV)

Asking and Receiving

People try to get their needs met in many ways. They might work hard for something. They might steal it. They may be jealous, so they fight for something that belongs to someone else. But none of these ways work. They still don't have what they want or need. Earlier, Jesus told his followers, "Until now you have asked for nothing in My name; ask and you will receive, so that your joy may be made full" (John 16:24 NASB). But often people don't ask God, and so they don't receive what they need.

Stephanie's parents were separated, and she moved with her mom to a new school district. She desperately wanted to make friends in her new school. She also needed some new clothes in a bigger size, but money had been very tight lately. She didn't want to add to her mom's money worries. Stephanie *wished* she had new friends and new clothes. Stephanie *hoped* she would make new friends and get new clothes. But nothing happened. Stephanie hadn't actually prayed and *asked God* for the things she needed.

Wishing isn't praying. Hoping isn't praying. Asking God to meet your needs is praying. Some people complain that God isn't answering their prayers, but they haven't actually asked God for anything! Couldn't God read your mind and give you what you need anyway? Yes—and sometimes he does. But he wants us to ask and receive. He wants us to talk to him about everything—including making a new friend and buying some jeans that fit. And his promise? "And my God will meet all your needs according to his glorious riches in Christ Jesus" (Philippians 4:19 NIV).

Do you "have not" because you "ask not"? Then talk to God right now. He wants to meet your needs.

Did You Know ...

if we're confused or don't know what to do, we can go right to God and ask for wisdom? See James 1:5.

More To Explore: Luke 11:9–10

Girl Talk:

How much time do you spend wishing and hoping for something? How much time do you spend asking God for what you need?

God Talk:

Lord, help me remember to ask you for everything. Thank you for providing the things I need. Amen.

Devotion #47

"Everyone born of God overcomes the world.
This is the victory that has overcome the world,
even our faith. Who is it that overcomes the
world? Only the one who believes that
Jesus is the Son of God."
—1 John 5:4–5 (TNIV)

Victory!

Every child of God can defeat the sin in her life and the evil
in the world. Believers who win these battles are the ones
who trust Christ to fight for them—and win!

Are you fighting a battle? Maybe you're a believer, but you
always blame your red hair and Irish ancestry for your terrible
temper. After exploding at people, you laugh it off. "After all,
I'm a hotheaded Irishman!" Lately, though, it isn't funny.
You lost two good friends after letting your anger spew
on them. Then you were kicked off the basketball
team for yelling at the coach and the referee.
Your hot temper beat you every time. If
you don't overcome it soon, you won't
have any friends left. You're tired of your
temper controlling your life. It's time to
fight back—and win. So you try, but
find it much harder than you expected.

We feel so weak and small, so how can we defeat the enemies inside us plus those around us in the world? Can we really be overcomers? *Yes*, because we're not doing the fighting. It's Jesus *in* us—fighting the war for us. "You, dear children, are from God and have overcome them, because the one who is in you is greater than the one who is in the world" (1 John 4:4 NIV). Satan sends his flaming arrows of doubt and fear, but Jesus blocks them all! And what should our attitude be? "But thanks be to God, who gives us the victory through our Lord Jesus Christ" (1 Corinthians 15:57 NKJV). Remember: victory is yours when you trust Christ to fight the battle.

Did You Know ...

overcoming the world means to "gain victory over its sinful ways of life," which is another way of describing obedience to God?

More To Explore: John 16:33

GirL TaLk:

What habits or temptations do you have trouble fighting? Have you tried letting Jesus defeat them *for* you? Can you give him the problem?

God TaLk:

Lord, I want to be someone who can defeat the enemies in my life. Thank you for fighting the battles for me. Amen.

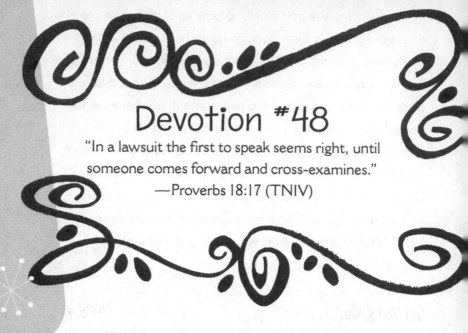

Devotion #48

"In a lawsuit the first to speak seems right, until someone comes forward and cross-examines."
—Proverbs 18:17 (TNIV)

Finding The Truth

When there is a fight or a dispute, you tend to believe the story of the person who tells her side first. It will sound so believable! Any story can sound true until someone else sets the record straight. You should hear both sides of a story before making up your mind.

Lindsey's locker partner was in tears after school. "You'll never believe what Trisha did!" her friend cried. Lindsey's friend described how Trisha had accused her of sticking her nose in Trisha's business. "She told me to butt out! I was only trying to help her with a problem!"

Lindsey listened with sympathy, wondering how Trisha could have been so mean. It was obvious that her locker partner had truly been trying to help Trisha deal with a boy who was bothering her. Lindsey decided to straighten Trisha out.

She did talk to Trisha, but it was Lindsey who got straightened out. It turned out that Trisha had been talking to Chad about their science project, when Lindsey's locker partner pushed in between them and dragged Chad aside, claiming she had a message for him. There was no message—she just wanted Chad's attention. Disgusted, Chad had shook her off and left the building with Trisha. After hearing both sides, Lindsey realized Trisha wasn't being mean at all.

Lindsey was glad she'd heard both sides before lecturing Trisha. That would have been embarrassing! "To answer before listening—that is folly and shame" (Proverbs 18:13 TNIV). Be sure to listen to both sides of a story or argument before forming an opinion. There are two sides to every story.

Did You Know ...

Joseph was thrown into prison for many years after being falsely accused by his master's wife? He was not allowed to tell his side of the story, but the Lord knew it, and he was with Joseph even in prison. He caused the prison guard to be kind to him until he was released.

More To Explore: Acts 25:16

Girl Talk:

Do you make up your mind quickly, without acquiring all the facts? How often do you end up being wrong?

God Talk:

Lord, I want to be calm when listening to someone's story. Help me keep an open mind till I hear both sides. Amen.

Devotion #49

"The law of the LORD is perfect, reviving
the soul. The statutes of the LORD are trustworthy,
making wise the simple . . . They are more
precious than gold, than much pure gold."
—Psalm 19:7, 10 (NIV)

Pure Gold

God's Word, our Bible, contains laws and principles for
believers to live by. These ideas for living can be trusted.
Even simpleminded people can be made wise by following
God's laws. God's Word is more valuable than twenty-four-
karat gold!

Perhaps you value something else, like acting. You want to
be a movie actress one day, and every waking minute you
can spare is spent watching movies, being in plays, and
memorizing lines. Sometimes you skip meals to practice
your lines. You miss football games with your
friends so you can go to voice lessons.

We all have things we consider valuable.
One girl might value her big house with a
swimming pool, while another girl might
value straight A's or a spot on the swim
team. David (who wrote many of the
psalms) thought God's Word, the Bible,

was the most valuable thing—even more valuable than gold. We also must learn to value God's Word above everything else we have.

How do you treat something that is valuable to you? You look at it. You spend time with it. You don't forget about it, but instead often put it first before everything else. We must treat God's Word that way. "And you must commit yourselves wholeheartedly to these commands I am giving you today . . . Talk about them when you are at home and when you are away on a journey, when you are lying down and when you are getting up again" (Deuteronomy 6:6–7 NLT). As we place a high value on God's Word, we'll see God change our lives in brand-new ways.

Did You Know ...

Job said God's Word was more important to him than food, and King David said it was more important than silver and gold? See Job 23:12 and Psalm 119:72.

More To Explore: Joshua 1:8

Girl Talk:

What do you value the most? How much time do you spend in this activity? How much time do you spend in God's Word?

God Talk:

Lord, you are the most important person in my life. Help me to put you first every day. Amen.

Fun Factoid:

Not every rock that glitters is gold. Some people are fooled by minerals with shiny golden flakes in them, and so the rocks are named "fool's gold."

Devotion #50

"I write these things to you who believe in the name of the Son of God so that you may know that you have eternal life." —1 John 5:13 (NIV)

Going My Way?

You don't ever have to wonder if you will go to heaven when you die. You can know for sure that you have eternal life. "So whoever has God's Son has life; whoever does not have his Son does not have life" (1 John 5:12 NLT). If you have accepted Jesus as your Savior—if you've accepted his forgiveness for your sins— you're going to heaven.

One summer when Melissa was ten years old, she'd prayed and asked for forgiveness during Bible school. Later, her sixth-grade teacher challenged her faith. He claimed that if God loved everyone equally, then everyone was a child of God and would go to heaven. Melissa knew he was wrong, but she couldn't put the reason into words. But that night, when digging into her Bible for answers, she found a familiar verse: "But as many as received Him, to *them* He gave the right to become children of God, even to those who believe in His name" (John 1:12 NKJV, emphasis added). Only those who receive Jesus are children of God.

Her uncle said that all the world's religions were the same, that they were just different ways to get to heaven. Again, Melissa went back to God's Word for answers. "Salvation is found in no one else, for there is no other name given under heaven by which we must be saved" (Acts 4:12 TNIV). And "Jesus answered, 'I am the way and the truth and the life. No one comes to the Father except through me'" (John 14:6 NIV). Melissa nodded. The Bible was clear. Salvation can be found only through Jesus.

For Melissa, that finally settled it. God said it—and she believed it.

Did You Know ...

anyone who refuses to believe in Jesus has called God a liar? See 1 John 5:10.

More To Explore: Romans 8:16

Girl Talk:

Do you know *why* you believe what you believe?

God Talk:

Lord, I want to know your Word better. Thank you that we can be *sure* we have eternal life. Amen.

Mini Quiz:

True or False? You know you're going to heaven if

A. you faithfully attend church.

B. you give large offerings.

C. you're kind to your enemies.

D. you accepted Jesus as your Savior.

(Answers: A. False; B. False; C. False; D. True)

Devotion #51

"Do not repay anyone evil for evil. Be careful to do what is right in the eyes of everybody."

—Romans 12:17 (NIV)

No Revenge

If someone does something mean or bad to you, you'll want to pay them back. But followers of Jesus never pay back evil for evil, not to anyone. Behave in such a way that anyone who is watching can see that you're honest and respectable.

Sometimes that's really hard. What if you receive a big red F on your science test? You can't believe it! You studied hard and were confident you'd earned an A. Under the F was a note from the teacher: "See me after class." You're totally unprepared for Mr. Fitch's words: "I never expected *you* to cheat. After the exam, Melanie reported you were copying from her test. Your answers were identical to hers." You sputter, "I didn't cheat!" Mr. Fitch scowls. "I'm sorry, but the evidence is against you. Why would Melanie lie about it?" You don't know why— but you intend to find out.

You charge out of the classroom and head toward the locker room. Melanie should still be there, changing for volleyball practice. Obviously Melanie copied *your* paper—then lied about it to cover her tracks. While storming down the hall, two verses pop into your mind. The verses irritate you—this is *not* what you want to hear. "Make sure that nobody pays back wrong for wrong, but always try to be kind to each other and to everyone else" (1 Thessalonians 5:15 NIV); and "Live such good lives among the pagans that, though they accuse you of doing wrong, they may see your good deeds and glorify God on the day he visits us" (1 Peter 2:12 NIV). Halfway down the hall, you change your mind about yelling at Melanie. You head home to cool off and pray about what to do.

Did You Know ...

in *Sophie's Stormy Summer*, Darbie learned how to react with love instead of hate when (back in Ireland) she was hit with eggs for being Catholic?

Girl Talk:

Have you ever been falsely accused of something? How did you handle it?

God Talk:

Lord, when you were mistreated, you never sinned in how you treated people. I want to be like you. Make me strong enough to follow your example. Amen.

More To Explore: 1 Peter 3:9 and Proverbs 20:22

Devotion #52

"All Scripture is inspired by God and is useful to teach us what is true and to make us realize what is wrong in our lives. It straightens us out and teaches us to do what is right."
—2 Timothy 3:16 (NLT)

Instruction Book

God's Word, from beginning to end, is true. God was actively involved in the writing of the Bible. He made us, and the Bible is our instruction manual. It teaches us how to live godly, successful lives. It is also useful to correct us when we take a wrong path.

Emily received a cell phone for her birthday, but she was soon so frustrated that she was ready to toss it in her desk drawer and leave it there. She couldn't program her friends' phone numbers into it. She couldn't figure out how to text-message. It was supposed to have a choice of ten different rings, but she couldn't get it to play the tune she wanted. Frustrated, she went to find her dad. "This thing doesn't work," Emily said. "It won't do anything right." Her dad took the phone and pressed a few buttons.

"Looks okay. Did you read the instruction book?" he asked.

In the same way that Emily needed to read the instruction manual for her cell phone, we need to read God's Word, our instructions for living. The Bible isn't just to carry to church on Sunday morning. In it, we have God's blueprint for our lives. It has the answer to every need we might have. His Word is sufficient for every circumstance we will ever face! But we need to read and study it. We need its wisdom every day if we want to make good decisions. And, like Emily, we need to both read the directions and *follow* them. "And remember, it is a message to obey, not just to listen to. If you don't obey, you are only fooling yourself" (James 1:22 NLT).

Dig into the Word today—and live right!

Did You Know ...

you can actually hide God's Word in your heart and be protected? See Psalm 119:11.

God Talk:

Lord, thank you for giving us your Word. Give me a real desire to read and obey it. Amen.

More To Explore: Proverbs 6:23

Girl Talk:

When you have a question about life or a problem to solve, whom do you ask for help? Do you go to God's Word for answers?

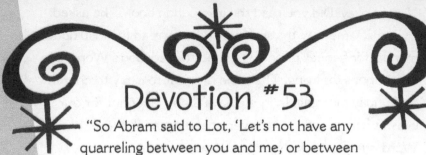

Devotion #53

"So Abram said to Lot, 'Let's not have any
quarreling between you and me, or between
your herdsmen and mine, for we are brothers.'"
—Genesis 13:8 (NIV)

Keeping The Peace

Abram was Lot's uncle, so they were close relatives.
But there wasn't enough land for everyone's flocks and
herds to live on. Abram stopped the fight before it could go
any further. He gave Lot first choice when they split the
land. Abram sacrificed the best land in order to keep peace
with his relative.

Like Abram, you may hate fighting. Maybe you hear it at
home nearly every night between your dad and your older
brother. Your brother's in trouble all the time: at school,
at his job, at home. When it starts up, you escape
to your room, close the door, and crank up
your music. Sometimes your brother even
tries to fight with you. He teases you, or
takes your homework, or calls you
names. You bite your tongue and pray,
refusing to take his bait. As hard as it is,
you know it's the right thing to do. "If it is

possible, as far as it depends on you, live at peace with everyone" (Romans 12:18 NIV). Always do what you can—which may involve leaving the room.

What if you're minding your own business, and someone else picks a fight with you? If they refuse to back off, is it then okay to let it rip and fight back? As tempting as that sounds, it would only backfire into more (and worse) fighting. "The Lord's servant must not be quarrelsome but must be kind to everyone, able to teach, not resentful" (2 Timothy 2:24 TNIV). You can't control someone else, but with God's help, you can control your own tongue. You can also walk away and not listen. "Blessed are the peacemakers, for they will be called children of God" (Matthew 5:9 TNIV).

Did You Know ...

friendships and families that are divided by constant strife and quarreling cannot survive, just as a house divided cannot stand? See Mark 3:24–25.

More To Explore:
Proverbs 17:14

Girl Talk:

Do you enjoy being around people who quarrel? Do you try to start quarrels or end them?

God Talk:

Lord, I want to be at peace with everyone. If someone tries to fight with me, help me to be quiet and walk away. Amen.

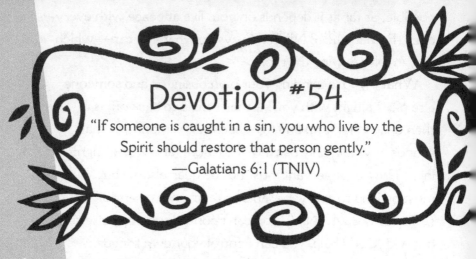

Devotion #54

"If someone is caught in a sin, you who live by the Spirit should restore that person gently."
—Galatians 6:1 (TNIV)

Support Each Other

Followers of Christ aren't perfect. They're forgiven. All believers have tests and trials, and sometimes we fail. If a fellow believer is caught in some sin, the other believers should confront her gently. Be humble. Don't pretend that you never make mistakes yourself.

Alyssa was shocked when she heard that Taylor, a girl in her youth group, was caught drinking with some older kids. When she spotted Taylor at school, Taylor turned red and walked the other way. Taylor skipped youth group Wednesday night, and Alyssa wished she could do something. Finally she decided to stop at Taylor's house on the way home. She had no idea what to say, but she wanted Taylor to know they wanted her back in youth group, no matter what. When Taylor opened the door, she blinked in surprise, then hung her head. "We missed you at group," Alyssa said. "Can we talk?" Taylor looked up, tears in her eyes. "Sure. Come on in."

If you're a follower of Jesus, you will have the same desire he does: "I will seek what was lost and bring back what was driven away, bind up the broken and strengthen what was sick" (Ezekiel 34:16 NKJV). If you can bring someone back from the path of bad decisions that will ruin her life, you're doing a wonderful thing. "If one of you should wander from the truth and someone should bring them back, remember this: Whoever turns a sinner from the way of error will save them from death and cover over a multitude of sins" (James 5:19–20 TNIV).

We all fail, and we all make mistakes. Instead of judging another believer, talk with her gently. Help her back on the right path. That's love in action.

Did You Know ...

Jesus compared believers who wandered away from God to lost sheep who needed to be found? See Matthew 18:12–15.

More To Explore: Matthew 9:13

Girl Talk:

Do you know a believer who is caught in some behavior that's wrong? How can you help? Are *you* caught in such behavior?

God Talk:

Lord, help me to not become prideful when someone else is caught doing something wrong. I want to have love for that person instead. Amen.

Devotion #55

"Friendship with the LORD is reserved for those who fear him. With them he shares the secrets of his covenant."—Psalm 25:14 (NLT)

God's Friend

You can be God's friend! Friendship with God is saved for those who fear or respect him. People who deeply respect the Lord arrange their lives according to his will. God takes such people into his confidence, sharing secrets with them about his promises.

You probably have one or two very good friends. They get to be your friends because they show respect to you. They respect your opinion, your time, your property, and your feelings. Because they treat you this way, you trust them and share many secrets with them—secrets you don't share with just anyone. You have no desire to share special things with people who make fun of your opinions or ignore your feelings.

God reveals special things to us too—if we respect him and obey his Word. If we are already doing what his Word says, we are his friends. And when we need special information (like "Should I go to this party?" or "Should I try out for the swim team?"), he will give it to us. Jesus told his disciples the same thing: "I no longer call you servants, because servants do not know their master's business. Instead, I have called you friends, for everything that I learned from my Father I have made known to you" (John 15:15 TNIV).

What could be more exciting than being friends with God and having him tell you secrets about himself, your life, and his many promises?

Did You Know ...

an unbeliever can't understand God's secrets—even if he wants to—because you need the Holy Spirit inside you to make God's words clear? See 1 Corinthians 2:14–15.

More To Explore: John 14:21

Girl Talk:

What kinds of friends do you like best? What kind of friend are you? Are you friends with God?

God Talk:

Lord, thank you for wanting to be my friend. I'm glad that we can share secrets with each other. Amen.

Mini Quiz:

Yes or No: Would a true friend do these things?
A. Stick up for you if someone gossiped about you
B. Tell your worst secret to another girl
C. Help you babysit on a Saturday night
D. Give you a hug when you cry

(Answers: A. Yes; B. No; C. Yes; D. Yes)

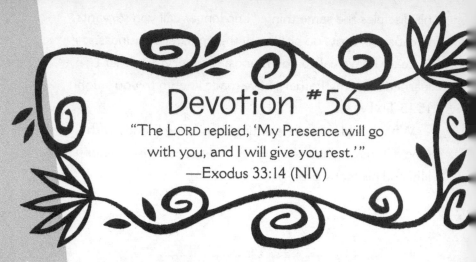

Devotion #56

"The LORD replied, 'My Presence will go
with you, and I will give you rest.'"
—Exodus 33:14 (NIV)

Never Alone

Moses was nervous about leading the Israelites into the Promised Land, but God told Moses not to worry. Why? Even though it would be a huge job, God promised to go with him. God himself would travel with Moses, and he would give Moses the rest he needed. Anna understood how Moses felt. She wasn't heading toward the Promised Land, but she and her family were moving clear across the country. Because of her dad's job transfer, she was leaving behind her friends, her school, her church, her 4-H group, even her horse. Everything familiar and loved was being left in Virginia, and everything in Oregon would be strange and new. When Anna finally told her mom how she felt about the move, her mom reminded her of one important fact. God was going with them, every step of the way. His presence would refresh them on their travels, and they'd be at peace when they arrived. God's presence would change everything.

If you're a follower of Jesus, you can be just as confident as Moses was when he led his people to the Promised Land. Jesus gives you this promise: "And surely I am with you always, to the very end of the age" (Matthew 28:20 NIV). Not only will Jesus be with you every step of the way along your journey, but he will provide refreshment for your weary body, mind, and emotions. "Then Jesus said, 'Come to me, all of you who are weary and carry heavy burdens, and I will give you rest'" (Matthew 11:28 NLT).

Just as God promised Moses, Jesus promises to be with you, guide you, and give you rest.

Did You Know ...

when God led the Israelites out of Egypt, his presence was with them in a very unique way as they walked through the desert? He led the way by day in a pillar of cloud. At night, a pillar of fire gave them light to see by. See Exodus 13:21.

More To Explore: Deuteronomy 31:7–8

Girl Talk:

Is God with you right now? How do you know? Can you always feel his presence?

God Talk:

Lord, thank you for always staying with me. Help me remember that I'm never alone. Amen.

Devotion #57

"Take no part in the worthless deeds of evil and darkness; instead, rebuke and expose them."
—Ephesians 5:11 (NLT)

No Way!

Don't have anything to do with people whose actions are morally wrong. Instead of joining in, confront those involved in such things. Make these deeds (which have been kept secret) known to the public.

Maybe you're shocked when your best friend admits she stole the semester test from the math teacher's desk and copied the answers before returning the test. Your friend offers the answers to you for free, although she plans to sell the answers to others in the class. "You can't do that!" you protest. "You know that's wrong!" Your friend laughs and says, "You're such a goody-goody. If you want a lower grade on the test, that's fine by me! I'm just looking out for myself." Disgusted, you turn and walk away.

You desperately wish you'd never discovered her plan. But you *do* know. What should you do with the information?

You're right in deciding not to participate in the stolen test answers. "I hate the gatherings of those who do evil, and I refuse to join in with the wicked"

(Psalm 26:5 NLT). Followers of Jesus should have no part in such activities, but are called to rebuke a person involved in something wrong. (You did that.) We should also make those actions public. You're sure your friend will hate you if you tell the teacher, and you don't want to be called a snitch. But after praying, reporting the scheme seems like the right thing to do. You arrive at school early the next morning and tell the math teacher about your friend's plan. He thanks you and says he will make up a new test. You wonder if your friend will know you blew the whistle. Maybe—but you feel at peace about your decision.

Did You Know ...

instead of being tolerant of sin, followers of Jesus are to "rebuke" and "exhort" fellow believers living sinful lives? (Titus 2:15 NKJV)

Girl Talk:

If you know kids are breaking the rules, is it ever okay to ignore it and walk away? What other things could you do?

God Talk:

Lord, I'm afraid to speak up when I see people doing wrong things. I'm afraid of what they'll say. Give me courage to say the words. Amen.

More To Explore: Romans 13:12 and Proverbs 4:14–15

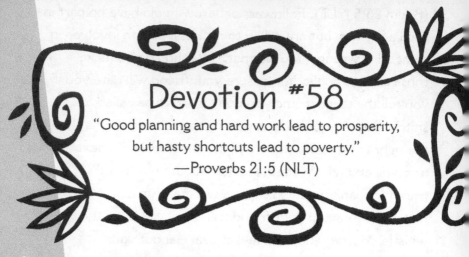

Devotion #58

"Good planning and hard work lead to prosperity,
but hasty shortcuts lead to poverty."
—Proverbs 21:5 (NLT)

Get Rich Quick?

The plans of those who quietly and steadily keep working are successful, and these hard workers have plenty. But people who take shortcuts or try to get rich quick miss their goals. They end up with few possessions and little money.

Amanda had spent all her allowance at the movies, but her dad's birthday was in a few days. She needed to make some money—fast! She decided to have a bake sale while he was at work on Saturday. Amanda didn't have all the ingredients for the cookie recipe, but she didn't think it would matter if she left out the eggs and baking powder. The dough looked—and tasted—normal without those things.

However, when she baked the balls of dough, they flattened into crusty chunks. No one wanted to buy them. Her shortcut backfired.

Even though hard work isn't as much fun as playing video games or going shopping, it's necessary if you want to be successful. Many people have to work in order to have the "extras" they want. Work teaches good habits—how to stick with a project, how to keep going until it's finished, and how to be a hard worker instead of a lazy person. "Lazy people are soon poor; hard workers get rich" (Proverbs 10:4 NLT). Poor or rich—which do you choose?

Did You Know ...

hard work is even necessary to be successful at something you love to do? Many girls in *Sophie Breaks the Code* try out for cheerleading—but the successful ones worked hard to win a place on the squad.

More To Explore: Proverbs 13:4

Girl Talk:

Do you like to work hard at some things, but not others? How do you feel at the end of a day when you have worked hard and finished a big project?

God Talk:

Lord, sometimes I don't like to work. Help me to plan well and work hard at all that I do. Amen.

Fun Factoid:

Even ants work hard. Many species of ants harvest seeds. These harvester ants, which are probably the ants noted in the Bible for their hard work, live in very dry parts of the world. They collect seeds and store them in special underground chambers for use when other types of food are scarce.

Devotion #59

"Then I said to them, 'You see the trouble we are in:
Jerusalem lies in ruins, and its gates have been
burned with fire. Come, let us rebuild the wall of
Jerusalem, and we will no longer be in disgrace."
—Nehemiah 2:17 (NIV)

FighT DiscouragemenT!

The wall around the city of Jerusalem had been broken
down, and the wooden gates had been burned. Those who
lived there were saddened by the condition of the city. But
Nehemiah prayed and called to them, saying, "Come! Let's
rebuild the wall!"

We too often have to rebuild. What if, after your parents'
divorce, your dad moves five states away? After that, you
see him only during the summer. Discouragement sets
in, and you quietly give up. Why try to have a
relationship with your dad when he lives so
far away? You confide in your best friend
that you plan to skip your next summer
visit—and why. Yes, your friend agrees,
the relationship with your dad has broken down. It's sad, but it doesn't have to

stay that way. "Come on. You can rebuild," your friend says. Together with your friend, you brainstorm some ways to heal the relationship with your dad. You start emailing him several times a week. You stay home when you know he plans to call. You learn how to use the family's digital camera and send him photos of your class trip, the opening night of your play, and some goofy shots with your friends. Within a few months, you feel a new closeness with him. "Arise, for this matter is your responsibility. We also will be with you. Be of good courage, and do it" (Ezra 10:4 NKJV).

It's easy to be down when you see things in ruins, whether it's your messy room or failing grades. Disappointments happen to everyone. But discouragement—when we lose confidence in ourselves, God, or others—*is a choice*. We can choose to be discouraged. Or we can do what Nehemiah did. We can study the situation and decide to rebuild.

Did You Know ...

during the rebuilding of the wall, the builders were mocked and threatened with attack, so they worked with one hand and carried a weapon in the other? See Nehemiah 4.

Girl Talk:

Are there things in your life that look ruined? In what ways can you begin to rebuild?

More To Explore: Isaiah 35:3–4

God Talk:

Lord, I choose not to be discouraged. Help me fix the broken things in my life. Thank you! Amen.

Devotion #60

"Make it your ambition to lead a quiet life, to
mind your own business and to work
with your hands, just as we told you."
—1 Thessalonians 4:11 (NIV)

M.Y.O.B.

Your goal should be to live a quiet life and mind your
own business. Don't be lazy or run around sticking your
nose into other people's personal matters. Instead, get a life!
Work hard at a job of your own.

Abby finished dressing in the locker room, then grabbed her
books and notebook. Glancing down, she frowned. Someone
had written big block letters on her notebook in marker. Fum-
ing, she showed her best friend on the way home. "What's
this mean, anyway?" Abby asked. She pointed to the letters: M.Y.O.B.!!!!!!!!!!! Joanie snickered. "It stands for
Mind Your Own Business." Abby stopped and
turned. "Why would anyone write *that* on
my notebook?" Joanie was silent, but
Abby poked her arm. "Answer me. Why
would someone write that? I'm not
nosy." Joanie finally told her the blunt
truth. "You're my best friend, Abby, but I

gotta say that you stick your nose into places where it doesn't belong." She mentioned how Abby had quizzed Samantha about her dad moving out. She recalled when Abby had grilled Chad about why he couldn't come to the class party. "And remember how red Suzanne got when you bugged her about not wearing a bra yet? That's none of your business. Lots of people could have written M.Y.O.B. on your notebook."

Is it really so bad to be curious and nose around in other people's lives? God thinks so. He lists being a busybody in the same sentence as some other very serious crimes! "But let none of you suffer as a murderer, a thief, an evil-doer, or as a busybody in other people's matters" (1 Peter 4:15 NKJV). It's wonderful to show true concern for other people's problems. But pushing people to share private things when they don't want to is just plain nosy. So learn to M.Y.O.B. People will love you for it!

Did You Know ...

a "Jack Horner" is another name for a busybody? (It's from the nursery rhyme "Little Jack Horner.") The term has come to mean someone who has to have a thumb in everyone else's pies.

More To Explore

Girl Talk:

Do you get so curious about others' lives that you meddle in their business? How do you feel when someone is nosy about *your* life?

God Talk:

Lord, I need to mind my own business. Help me to pray for others instead. Amen.

1 Timothy 5:13 and 2 Thessalonians 3:11

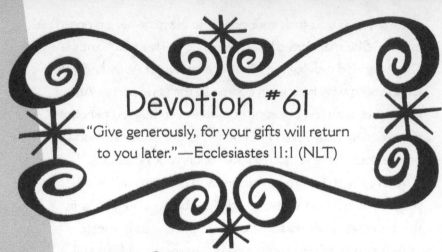

Devotion #61

"Give generously, for your gifts will return to you later."—Ecclesiastes 11:1 (NLT)

Freely Give

Giving generously means giving more than is convenient. It's not being stingy, or just giving the leftovers you don't need. Generous giving is giving *big* with a willing heart and an open hand. You will be blessed by God for being a generous giver.

If you watched the tsunami and Hurricane Katrina coverage on TV, you were probably heartbroken at the staggering needs shown. You knew your parents and church donated money to the relief efforts, but you wanted to make a difference yourself. So you organized your friends to do a weekend car wash and bake sale, and made sure the customers knew that 100 percent of the proceeds would be sent to the victims. You were able to raise over a hundred dollars to donate. Even though you wouldn't give the money just so you'd feel better, it *did* give you a lot of satisfaction. "The generous will themselves be blessed, for they share their food with the poor" (Proverbs 22:9 TNIV).

God takes what you give and makes it grow and multiply. Proverbs 11:25 (TNIV) says, "A generous person will prosper; whoever refreshes others will be refreshed." Your gifts help others, and what you receive back will surprise you. "Remember this: Whoever sows sparingly will also reap sparingly, and whoever sows generously will also reap generously" (2 Corinthians 9:6 NIV). Everything you have comes from the Lord. It's not really yours, so don't hang on to it with an iron grip. Instead, give generously and watch the blessings flow—both ways!

Did You Know ...

if you are kind to the poor, God says he will bless you, help you out of trouble, protect you, honor you, destroy the power of your enemies, and nurse you when you're sick? See Psalm 41:1–3.

God Talk:

Lord, I think of myself too much. Help me to be generous with others today—and every day. Amen.

More To Explore: Hebrews 6:10

Girl Talk:

What kinds of things could you give to help someone else? Do you have a talent you could share? Are there needy people in your own church or neighborhood (like single moms who could use free babysitting)? What could you give today?

"You Made My Day"

When you love, you give a gift,
And when you're gone—it stays.
It's passed on by the ones you loved
To make another's day.

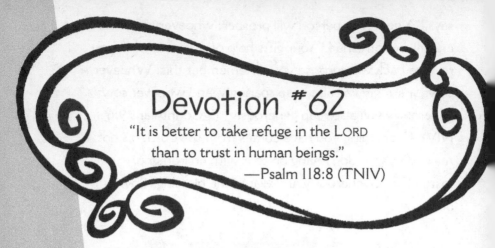

Devotion #62

"It is better to take refuge in the LORD
than to trust in human beings."
—Psalm 118:8 (TNIV)

Whom Can You Trust?

Only God is perfect and will never let you down.
Put your trust in him, not in people. People can't
help it; even the most loving person will sometimes
fail you. However, God is completely trustworthy.
Kelsey had a rotten day at school. She flunked a math
test, twisted her ankle in gym, and the boy she liked asked
the new girl to the after-game dance. Kelsey wanted to crawl
into a hole and disappear. Thank heavens for her best friend,
Shayna. What would she do without her? Shayna always called
right after supper. Kelsey couldn't wait to pour out her heart
and get some much-needed comfort. But seven o'clock
passed, then eight, then nine. It was nearly ten before
Shayna called, and then only to say that she'd gone
shopping and to a movie with her mom, and she
just got home, and she couldn't talk! In tears,
Kelsey curled up on her bed. How could
Shayna have let her down like that? Cry-
ing, Kelsey did what would have helped
in the first place. She poured out her hurt
to God. "Trust in him at all times, O
people; pour out your hearts to him, for
God is our refuge" (Psalm 62:8 NIV).

Kelsey made a common mistake. She put Shayna in the place of God, and of course, Shayna let her down. People are human. They aren't God. People can't always be there for us, even when they want to be. Sometimes people are self-centered or even mean. Most friends do the best they can, but it's a mistake to put our wholehearted trust in them. Instead, put that trust in the Lord. "Blessed are those who make the LORD their trust" (Psalm 40:4 TNIV). So take the pressure off your friends. Lean hard on the Lord instead.

Did You Know ...

the Bible says the Lord is a *refuge* (a shelter from danger or hardship) in times of trouble? See Nahum 1:7.

GirL TaLk:

Who is the person you trust the most? How can you build up your trust in God?

God TaLk:

Lord, thank you for showing me that you alone deserve my total trust. Help my faith in you to grow. Amen.

More To Explore: Jeremiah 17:5, 7

Devotion #63

"Test everything. Hold on to the good."
—1 Thessalonians 5:21 (NIV)

Testing! Testing!

Don't believe everything you hear. Ask questions, check it out, and see if it can be proved. "Dear friends, do not believe everyone who claims to speak by the Spirit. You must test them to see if the spirit they have comes from God. For there are many false prophets in the world" (1 John 4:1 NLT).

You honestly want to do what God wants, but sometimes you have trouble recognizing his voice. Is it God or just your own ideas? You can't test those voices until you know God better. You may think of him as an angry judge—until you read: "Therefore, there is now no condemnation for those who are in Christ Jesus" (Romans 8:1 NIV). You're not sure you can count on God—until you read: "And surely I am with you always, to the very end of the age" (Matthew 28:20 NIV). The better you get to know God, the easier it is to recognize his still, small voice. "Do not conform any longer to the pattern of this world, but be transformed by the renewing of your mind" (Romans 12:2

NIV). Consistent reading and study of the Bible will renew *your* mind. Knowing God's truth will help you recognize the lies you'll hear in the world. It's like learning anything new. Before you could add, if someone had claimed that two plus two equaled five, you probably would have believed her. You wouldn't know any different. But once you learned your addition tables, if someone told you that two plus two equaled five, you'd spot the lie. You'd know the truth by then—that two plus two equals four.

In the same way, you can spot the lies of the world and the devil by filling your mind more and more with God's truth. Test everything. Compare what you hear to the Word of God.

Did You Know ...

in the Bible, false prophets are called ravenous wolves dressed up to look like harmless sheep? See Matthew 7;15.

Girl Talk:

Do you believe everything you hear? How can you use the Bible to discover whether people are telling the truth?

More To Explore: Acts 17:11

God Talk:

Lord, thank you for the Bible that teaches me the truth. Help me to go to it for answers first. Amen.

Devotion #64

"When [Jesus] saw the crowds, he had compassion
on them, because they were harassed and helpless,
like sheep without a shepherd."
—Matthew 9:36 (NIV)

Lost Sheep

Jesus went through all the towns and villages, teaching
and preaching and healing the sick. Everywhere he went,
people came to him with their problems. They were in distress and pain, helpless to fix their own problems. To Jesus,
they seemed lost, like sheep wandering the hillside without a
shepherd to care for them. He had deep pity for their suffering and wanted to help them.

Megan was chatting with her best friend, Nora, when
she noticed a girl on crutches approaching the school.
The girl caught her crutch on a chunk of pro-
truding cement and dropped her books.

Nora laughed and grabbed Megan's arm.
"Did you hear how that happened? She
sprained her ankle trying to skateboard
with some little kids. What a loser."
Megan hesitated, then shook off her

friend's hand and hurried to help the girl pick up her books. She carried her bag into the school for her.

As believers, we must not be critical of someone else's struggles. God wants to use you to help others. If you're critical instead of kind, you're useless. We are called to love one another. The only time you are to ever look *down* upon someone is when you're bending over to help them *up*. Look around you today with a loving, compassionate eye. Who could use your help?

Did You Know ...

the people of Israel are often described in the Bible as sheep scattered without a shepherd? See Numbers 27:17; 1 Kings 22:17; 2 Chronicles 18:16.

More To Explore: Isaiah 40:11

Girl Talk:

When your classmates have trouble or sickness or problems, how do you respond? Do you gossip about them? Or do you try to help them?

God Talk:

Lord, I don't want to criticize someone for having a problem. Show me how I can help instead. Amen.

Beauty 101:

For a description of true beauty, read about the kind, compassionate woman in Proverbs 31: "She extends a helping hand to the poor and opens her arms to the needy" (v. 20 NLT). Compassion makes a person beautiful, and it doesn't fade like physical beauty. "Charm is deceptive, and beauty does not last; but a woman who fears the LORD will be greatly praised" (v. 30 NLT).

Devotion #65

"The LORD demands fairness in every
business deal; he sets the standard."
—Proverbs 16:11 (NLT)

Me, a Cheater?

It can be tempting to cut corners to make a bigger
profit, or to charge more for a job than is honest.
God sets the standard in business as in all other
parts of life. The standard is total honesty.

If someone accuses you of cheating, you would be
horrified and hurt. You don't cheat! You study hard and
never get answers to test questions in any dishonest way.
You always do your chores for which you're paid an
allowance. So how could you cheat? On your part-time job,
that's where. You babysit the neighbor's two small children
after school. You're paid for two hours of work each afternoon: helping with homework, making them a healthy
snack, and playing with them. In truth, seven-eighths
of the time you "babysit," you chat on the phone
with your best friend. The kids make their
own (junky) snacks and plop down in front
of the TV. Fifteen minutes before their
mom is due home, you hang up, turn
off the TV, make the kids change
clothes and get out their homework. By
the time their mom arrives home, you're

all seated at the dining room table, hard at work. Every day you're paid for two hours of work, yet you *work* only fifteen minutes.

How does God view that? "The LORD hates cheating, but he delights in honesty" (Proverbs 11:1 NLT). Honesty and trustworthiness are important character traits for Christians to develop. Cheating people in business—getting paid for work you haven't done—dishonors the Lord and those who hire you. Make a promise to yourself and God today. Be determined to be honest in all your business dealings.

Did You Know ...

the most common weight in Bible times was the shekel? Of all Jewish weights, the shekel was the most accurate. Dishonest merchants had scales that weighed incorrectly so they could cheat customers. The Lord had a lot to say about such people who used "differing weights and differing measures."

More To Explore: Proverbs 20:10

Girl Talk:

Do you have jobs for which you are paid? Are you honest about how much work you actually do?

God Talk:

Lord, I want to be excellent in all I do. Help me to always be fair to someone who pays me for work I do. Amen.

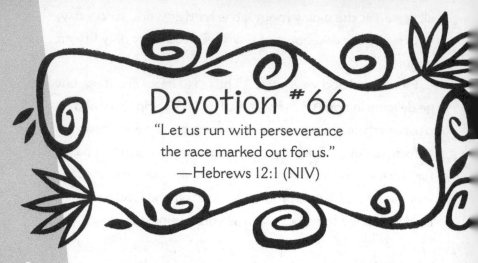

Devotion #66

"Let us run with perseverance
the race marked out for us."
—Hebrews 12:1 (NIV)

Sticking To IT

The Christian life is pictured as a long-distance race rather than a short sprint. It takes a combination of patience, endurance, and persistent determination to finish the race.

Lauren was a long-distance runner on the school track team. She dreamed of running a marathon someday. Her main event in the spring was the 1,500-meter run; she also ran cross-country in the fall. She was small, like many endurance runners she'd read about or watched on TV. Lauren ran on the days she didn't want to, the days it rained, the days her shins hurt, and the days she had plans with her friends. She ran first. In the races themselves, she regulated her speed carefully to avoid tiring too soon. She saved enough energy for the "kick," a sprint for the finish line on the last lap. But to Lauren, the most important thing she did to win was run with Leah. Leah cheered her on, waited at the end of the runs with water and a shoulder to lean on, and picked Lauren up a few times when she fell.

The important thing is to finish the race of life and find (and fulfill) God's purpose for your life. God understands that we will stumble and fall sometimes. We don't need to run the race perfectly—or alone. Jesus makes sure we never run solo. He goes ahead of us to clear a path and behind us to pick us up when we fall. He runs beside us to encourage us.

To be successful in your life, cultivate the quality of endurance. "But the seed on good soil stands for those with a noble and good heart, who hear the word, retain it, and by persevering produce a crop" (Luke 8:15 NIV).

Did You Know ...

in the sprints, short hurdles races, long jump, and triple jump, any wind that might help a competitor's perform- ance is measured? If the wind exceeds 2.0 meters (or 6 feet, 6 inches) per second, then the mark cannot be considered for record purposes.

More To Explore: Matthew 24:13

Girl Talk:

What in your life do you need endurance for? Where do you find it?

God Talk:

Lord, I want to finish my race with fly- ing colors. Thank you for running it with me. Amen.

Devotion #67

"But if you keep looking steadily into God's perfect law—the law that sets you free—and if you do what it says and don't forget what you heard, then God will bless you for doing it."
—James 1:25 (NLT)

Don't Forget!

If you read and study God's Word and then do what it says, your life will be happy. But you can't just pay attention for a while and then forget all about it. Follow through with obedience if you want God's blessings in your life.

In Sunday school, your class is studying the tongue. You know the tongue can be used for good (encouraging others) or evil (gossiping and backbiting). You've memorized several verses about it. Yet, when you're with your friends on Monday, you join them in cutting down some girls who tried out for cheerleader. Later in the restroom, you overhear your friends cutting *you* down! You can't believe it! You shouldn't be surprised, though. People who gossip tend to get gossiped about in return. You need to do more than memorize verses about the tongue. You need to put them into practice.

God is a good God and wants to bless his children. We must understand that disobedience can never be rewarded. Rebellion brings only discipline and negative consequences. If you want to please God and receive all that he wants to give you, then you must choose obedience to his perfect law. "If you keep My commandments, you will abide in My love, just as I have kept My Father's commandments and abide in His love. These things I have spoken to you, that My joy may remain in you, and that your joy may be full" (John 15:10–11 NKJV). What bigger reward for obedience could there be than this?

Don't just mentally agree with God's Word. Get out in the world and really live it!

Did You Know ...

Jesus said that whoever hears his sayings and obeys them is like a person who builds a house on solid rock? (See Luke 6:47–49.) Base your life on the teachings of Jesus, and *your* feet will be on solid ground.

More To Explore: John 13:17

Girl Talk:

Do you read your Bible and find areas of your life that need to be straightened out? Do you confess the sin and choose to obey? Or do you shrug it off and live the same as always?

God Talk:

Lord, I want to be a *doer* of your Word, and not just a hearer only. I need your help! Amen.

Devotion #68

"The LORD came and stood there, calling as at the other times, 'Samuel! Samuel!' Then Samuel said, 'Speak, for your servant is listening.'"
—1 Samuel 3:10 (NIV)

Who's That?

At first, Samuel couldn't tell who was calling to him in the middle of the night. Finally he realized it was God trying to talk to him! Samuel did the only smart thing possible. He closed his mouth and listened. When God speaks to us, we should do likewise! But how do we recognize his voice? Monica felt a nudge, almost a gentle whisper inside, when she first met the girl in the apartment next door. Monica hoped they could be friends and walk to school together, since they were in the same grade. However, her internal alarm whispered, "Don't trust her." The following week Monica overheard the girl lie to her mother about where she'd been. Later, after the girl visited Monica's apartment, some money was missing from her room. Was the funny feeling in her stomach the Lord trying to warn Monica about her new friend?

We must be alert and notice when God is trying to get our attention. Remember when God talked to Moses from within the burning bush? Moses could have been so self-focused that he never noticed the bush off to the side. But Moses was paying attention. "So when the LORD saw that he turned aside to look, God called to him from the midst of the bush and said, 'Moses, Moses!' And he said, 'Here I am'" (Exodus 3:4 NKJV).

Invite God to speak to you. Like Moses, pay attention to your surroundings. Like Samuel, perk up your ears and say, "Talk to me, Lord. I'm listening."

Did You Know ...

when Saul heard the voice of the Lord (see Acts 22:7–8), he turned from persecuting Christians and (with his new name, Paul) began telling others about Jesus? He heard the Lord's directions—and he obeyed them.

More To Explore: Genesis 22:11

Girl Talk:

Does God speak to you? How do you experience his voice? How can you know it's him?

God Talk:

Lord, I can't run my life without you. I need to hear from you every day. Please teach me how to hear you even better. Amen.

Beauty 101:

Clean those ears! We have earwax to prevent dust and other tiny particles from entering the ear's passage-way. However, too much wax in your ear can, in fact, decrease your hearing.

Devotion #69

"Be strong and courageous. Do not be terrified;
do not be discouraged, for the LORD your God will
be with you wherever you go."—Joshua 1:9 (NIV)

Mega Courage

Because God is with you, you can be strong and
brave. With God on your side, you're able to face
and deal with danger or fear without pulling back.
Since God is with you, there's no need to tremble or be
dismayed or lose hope.

Suppose you wave good-bye to your mom and follow the
stewardess into the plane. Hopefully your legs will hold you
up till you find your seat. You're flying—alone—to spend the
summer with your dad and his new wife in Colorado. You've
never been so scared in your life. What if you have to sit by
a really weird guy the whole trip? What if Crissy, your
new stepmom, doesn't like you? You've been warned
about wicked stepmothers! What if you hate the
town, the house, your room? You buckle your
seat belt, blink back tears, and peer out the
tiny window. You miss your mom so
much already.

While taxiing to the runway, you dig
in your backpack. What's that? You pull
out a small package with your mom's

handwriting on it: "Read this if you're afraid." It's a tiny pink Bible. In it is a card with verses. You read eagerly: "The LORD is my light and my salvation—whom shall I fear? The LORD is the stronghold of my life—of whom shall I be afraid?" (Psalm 27:1 NIV); and "I am with you and will watch over you wherever you go, and I will bring you back to this land. I will not leave you until I have done what I have promised you" (Genesis 28:15 NIV). Many times during the flight—and during the summer—you read God's Word for courage. Your strength increases as you grow to believe that God's in total control of everything you face. You can have that confidence every day!

Did You Know ...

God promises to be with you even if you have to walk through rushing rivers and hot flames? (See Isaiah 43:1–2.) He says the water won't overflow you nor will you even be scorched!

More To Explore: Joshua 1:6–7

Girl Talk:

What things frighten you? Do you believe God is in total control of those scary situations?

God Talk:

Lord, thank you that I can get my courage and strength from you. Help me to always remember that. Amen.

145

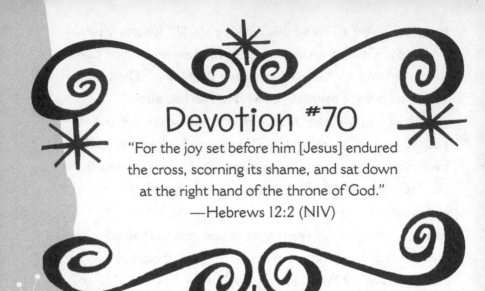

Devotion #70

"For the joy set before him [Jesus] endured
the cross, scorning its shame, and sat down
at the right hand of the throne of God."
—Hebrews 12:2 (NIV)

Focus!

Jesus was able to die a tortured death on the cross
because he focused on the joy he knew would be his after
it was over. In order to endure the pain, he directed his
attention to the reward that would come later: being seated
in the place of highest honor beside God's throne in heaven.

We, too, often need to focus on the future. Melissa planned
to run in a 10K race to help raise money for an orphanage,
and it took daily focus for months to train for that race.

Pete was saving money for a minibike, and every week
he had to say no to something his friends wanted to
do that would cost the money he was saving.

Renee wanted a part in the musical, and
she practiced daily through exhaustion
and sore throats in order to compete. All
three were successful—but only
because they found the power to focus
on their goals and not get sidetracked.

Jesus is our greatest example of the power of focus. Life will bring many tests and problems our way. Only those who put their attention on the promises in God's Word will survive and have a joyful life. Focus on God's ability—not your problem. He promises to work everything out for your good (see Romans 8:28), so concentrate on that good result expected at the end. If you're dealing with a problem (like a bully at school or your parents splitting up), you may not know how God is going to work it out. So simply focus on the fact that God is in control and has a good plan for you. God will give you the strength to see it through!

Did You Know ...

the highest number of gold medals ever won at one Olympics is seven? Mark Spitz, an American swimmer, first competed in the Olympics in 1968. Four years later, he won seven gold medals, a feat unbeaten by any athlete.

More To Explore: Philippians 3:13–14

Girl Talk:

What hard thing are you dealing with now? Would focusing on the result you want help you get through it?

God Talk:

Lord, I want to be more like Jesus. Help me to concentrate on the victory at the end. Amen.

Devotion #71

"But don't begin until you count the cost. For who
would begin construction of a building without
first getting estimates and then checking to
see if there is enough money to pay the bills?"
—Luke 14:28 (NLT)

Counting The Cost

When Jesus talked to the people about becoming his followers, he warned them that it could be costly. Jesus didn't want his followers to expect only blessings. Jesus knew that being his disciple would come at a price—even though the price would always be worth it. His disciples would have to give up some things. He wanted them to first consider the cost and what he expected of them before they committed their lives to him. "Count the cost" is good advice before committing to *any* new activity. In some cases, the price might be too high.

You might be thrilled when a neighbor lady asks if you will babysit her children two hours after school each day, plus all day Saturday. You calculate quickly. That'd be eighteen hours every week, at four dollars an hour! Your head is spinning.

You'll be able to buy all the clothes you want and get that new CD. You can buy some great Christmas gifts for your family. Your parents say you can make the decision for yourself, but first they sit down with you to count the cost. Being tied up after school means no sports during the year, since your volleyball and track teams practice after school. It would also mean no hanging out with friends on Saturday. Sundays would have to be spent on homework. Is it a price you're willing to pay, week after week, all through the school year? In the end, after counting the cost, you decide the cost is too high and turn down the job. You decide that there are more important things in your life than what money can buy.

Whenever you start a project or a new job, hold back your enthusiasm long enough to plan ahead. Make sure that you can carry it through.

Did You Know ...

Jesus told his disciples that one of the costs of following him would be having no home? "And Jesus said to him, 'Foxes have holes and birds of the air have nests, but the Son of Man has nowhere to lay His head'" (Matthew 8:20 NKJV).

More To Explore: Proverbs 7:23

Girl Talk:

Do you jump into things without thinking? How does that usually work out for you?

God Talk:

Lord, I need to be patient when taking on new projects. Give me wisdom to make good decisions. Amen.

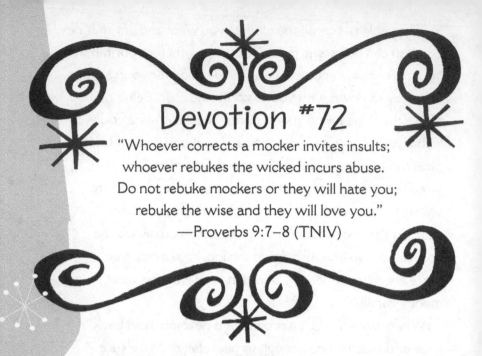

Devotion #72

"Whoever corrects a mocker invites insults;
whoever rebukes the wicked incurs abuse.
Do not rebuke mockers or they will hate you;
rebuke the wise and they will love you."
—Proverbs 9:7–8 (TNIV)

Becoming Wiser and Wiser

If you try to correct someone who jeers and sneers and treats things with contempt, you'll probably receive rude, nasty remarks for your effort. If you scold or lecture a morally wrong person, you'll likely receive abuse and cruel treatment in return. Don't bother scolding a mocker—he will just hate you. Correct a wise person, though, and she'll love you.

Lisa babysat for the Wilson family's three small children. When Mrs. Wilson arrived home early one day, Lisa was on the phone with a girlfriend and hadn't even realized that the youngest napping child had crawled out of bed and gone outside. When Mrs. Wilson asked her to not take personal calls anymore while babysitting, Lisa erupted. She slammed down the phone, swore, and scowled at Mrs. Wilson. That was the end of her babysitting job!

The new babysitter, Samantha, needed correction too. She fed the children too many sweets. Her response when corrected? "I'm sorry, Mrs. Wilson. I'll do better from now on." And she did. Eventually she was given a raise in wages.

"Whoever loves discipline loves knowledge, but whoever hates correction is stupid" (Proverbs 12:1 TNIV). That's pretty blunt—but it's true. If you want to be wiser, you'll listen to correction and take the discipline. It's stupid to make the same mistakes—and pay for them—over and over again. "Do not be like a senseless horse or mule that needs a bit and bridle to keep it under control" (Psalm 32:9 NLT).

Did You Know ...

the various kinds of bits for a horse's mouth can be used to communicate gently with the horse (guiding him and giving directions), or the bits can be used in such a way that the horse is forced to respond in order to avoid pain?

More To Explore: Proverbs 13:1; 15:12

Girl Talk:

If you were a horse, what kind of bit would you need in your mouth? Do you respond to simple directions, or do you have to be forced into obedience?

God Talk:

Lord, it's embarrassing to be corrected, and sometimes it hurts. Help me to listen to correction and learn from it. Amen.

Devotion #73

Good people bring good things out of the good stored up in them, and evil people bring evil things out of the evil stored up in them." —Matthew 12:35 (TNIV)

Treasure Hunt

You can't tell by studying a person's looks if she is good or bad. Watch the person's actions instead. Someone with a good heart will say and do kind things. But watch out for the person with an evil heart! Have you ever been unhappy with your best friends? You want to hang with them, but you get your feelings hurt a lot. They tease you about your haircut, your flat chest, and your big nose. Even though they claim they're just kidding, you feel ugly and gawky when around them. They *say* they're your friends, but their actions don't match their words. You finally admit to yourself that your "friends" are mean-spirited and hard-hearted. You decide to make new friends—this time with girls who act kind, as real friends should.

Where our hearts go, our lives will follow. If you store up good things in your heart, good things will come out of you. That includes godly words and kind actions. If you store up evil things, then that's what will come out of you. There's an easy way to discover the condition of your heart (or someone else's). Just check out your daily actions. Whatever appears on the outside, first took place on the inside.

If someone gave your heart a checkup, what kind of treasure would they find? Be sure you're filling your heart with God's Word. Then you'll have treasure that you (and others around you) will cherish.

Did You Know ...

Jesus called the Pharisees a bunch of snakes? He was tired of their phony behavior. "You brood of vipers, how can you who are evil say anything good? For out of the overflow of the heart the mouth speaks" (Matthew 12:34 TNIV).

More To Explore: Psalm 37:30–31

Girl Talk:

Do you know what is stored in your heart? How can you tell? Take time to examine your heart. Is it taking you where you want to go?

God Talk:

Lord, help me be more careful about what gets stored in my heart. I only want good things coming out of me. Amen.

Devotion #74

"Your approval or disapproval means nothing to me, because I know you don't have God's love within you." —John 5:41–42 (NLT)

People Pleasing

Jesus was often criticized, but the approval of people meant nothing to him. His unwavering confidence in God's approval set him free from human opinion. It can also free you from the trap of "people pleasing."

Nicole's youth group at church was having a lock-in Friday night. Nicole had a starring role in the evening's opening skit, and she looked forward to it. That is, until Kaylie invited her to a skating party for the same night. Kaylie was the most popular girl in Nicole's grade and rarely spoke to Nicole. Now she'd been invited to a party with Kaylie's friends! Nicole desperately wanted to go. What would Kaylie think of her if she turned down a party invitation to go to church? Nicole hedged and said she'd let Kaylie know the next day. That night, Nicole wrestled with her emotions. She wanted Kaylie to like her, but she'd promised to be in the skit at the lock-in. She knew without even praying that God wouldn't approve if she skipped the lock-in in favor of pleasing Kaylie. It was hard turning down the party invitation, but in the end, pleasing God mattered more to Nicole.

Jesus had some hard words of warning on this subject: "No wonder you can't believe! For you gladly honor each other, but you don't care about the honor that comes from God alone" (John 5:44 NLT). If you live to earn the rewards that come from pleasing people, you create a trap for yourself. No matter what you do, not everyone will approve of you. Even your best friends won't be pleased with you all the time. If, instead, you concentrate on receiving *God's* approval, you can live free from the trap of human opinion.

Did You Know ...

Jesus received God's praise and approval when God called down from heaven, "This is my beloved Son; I am fully pleased with him" (2 Peter 1:17 NLT).

GirL TaLk:

When you have to make a decision, whose approval matters the most to you? Your own? A friend's? Your parents'? God's?

More To Explore: 1 Thessalonians 2:6

God TaLk:

Lord, help me look to you for my approval. If my actions and attitudes please you, that's all that matters. Amen.

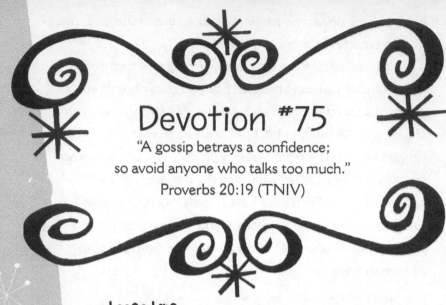

Devotion #75

"A gossip betrays a confidence;
so avoid anyone who talks too much."
Proverbs 20:19 (TNIV)

Loose Lips

Never choose a gossip for a friend. Such a person tells secrets. Don't hang around with someone who reveals private information that should not be passed on. What if your dad loses his job when the failing company he works for cuts back on employees? Things get tough at home, but your dad's unemployment isn't overly painful for you until you hear the gossip at school. Someone has spread a story that your dad was fired for punching his boss, and he's going to jail! You're hurt, shocked, and humiliated. You never do track down the source of the gossip. It's months before the story stops being repeated. Only when your dad finds another job—instead of being arrested—does the gossip die.

Sadly, there are people who pretend to be your friends, using smooth talk and flattery to persuade you to reveal your secrets. They like to be "in the know" and enjoy being the first one to spread a story. Gossip creates harsh disagreements that often force a group of friends to split and take sides. This is *not* the kind of people you want for friends. "Watch out for those who cause divisions . . . Keep away from them" (Romans 16:17 NIV).

What kind of people should you surround yourself with? "Gossips betray a confidence, but the trustworthy keep a secret" (Proverbs 11:13 TNIV). How can you know who's trustworthy? Test her. Tell her a small secret and wait. Does she keep it to herself? If so, try revealing something more personal. Again, wait a week or two. Does your secret get spread around? Trust and reveal more a little bit at a time. There are trustworthy people you can have for friends. Search for them, but avoid the gossips.

Did You Know ...

gossip is cruel? It makes innocent people cry. Even the word *gossip* hisses. Before you repeat a story, ask yourself: *Is it true? Is it harmless? Is it necessary?*

More To Explore: Proverbs 26:20-22

GirL TaLk:

Are you a gossip? Do you give in to the temptation to tell secrets about other people?

God TaLk:

Lord, I don't want to gossip. Take control of what I say and keep my lips sealed. See Psalm 141:3 (NLT).

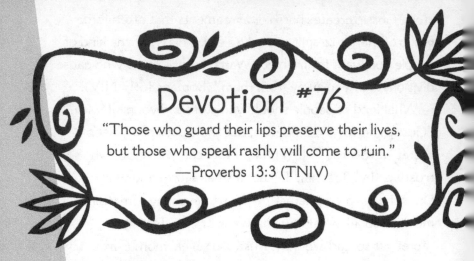

Devotion #76

"Those who guard their lips preserve their lives,
but those who speak rashly will come to ruin."
—Proverbs 13:3 (TNIV)

Zipeth Thy Lip!

The tongue holds the power of life and death,
according to Proverbs 18:21. The ability to control
the tongue is a clear sign of wisdom. The person who
keeps watch over her mouth keeps her life from unnec-
essary harm. On the other hand, speaking in a hasty and
foolhardy manner can end up ruining your life. Use of the
tongue in speaking can have powerful positive *or* negative
consequences!

Jasmine was outspoken, and she had always viewed being
that way as a positive thing. After all, people could trust her
to be honest. Brutally so, sometimes. If she didn't like her
friend's hair or clothing, she told her. If she disagreed
with her math teacher and was positive she was
right, she spoke up and corrected him. However, over time, she noticed her friend
avoided her, preferring to hang with girls
Jasmine considered mousy nerds. And
her teacher noted on her report card
that Jasmine was "bright, but argumen-
tative." Jasmine finally admitted to herself

that speaking without thinking was costly—and she decided to make some changes.

There's nothing wrong with being honest. In fact, the Bible says we are to speak the truth—but in love (see Ephesians 4:15). You can be honest, yet kind and tactful at the same time. Sometimes we simply chatter on and on, though, without having anything important to say. In that case, "don't talk too much, for it fosters sin. Be sensible and turn off the flow!" (Proverbs 10:19 NLT).

Remember what a powerful force your tongue is. Don't ruin your own life by letting your tongue go wild. Get it under control and find real freedom.

Did You Know ...

many countries have sayings about how powerful the tongue is?

- "The tongue has no bones, yet it breaks bones." (Greek)
- "The tongue of a bad friend cuts more than a knife." (Spanish)

More To Explore: Proverbs 21:23

Girl Talk:

When do you have the most trouble controlling your tongue? Is it when you hang around certain people? Can you create a plan so that doesn't happen again?

God Talk:

Lord, help me guard my tongue and keep quiet unless I have something helpful to say. Amen.

Devotion #77

"I have hidden your word in my heart that
I might not sin against you."
—Psalm 119:11 (NIV)

What Are You Eating?

Whatever is saved or stored in your heart will
guide and direct your life. You will live out the
beliefs you have deep down. So it's important to
feed your heart with God's Word. That will control
your actions and keep you from sinning.

Suppose your mom remarries, and when the two families are combined, you have to share your bedroom with a
younger stepsister. The little girl irritates you with her questions and nonstop chatter. Your mom begs you to be patient
with your new sibling, and you do feel guilty when you snap
at the little girl and make her cry. Yet you can't gain control
over your tongue. Your feelings always take over.

Then you hear at Sunday school that memorizing
God's Word can keep you from acting on those
impulses. You're doubtful, but you try it anyway. You memorize verses about the
tongue: "Those who guard their mouths
and their tongues keep themselves from
calamity" (Proverbs 21:23 TNIV). "She
opens her mouth with wisdom, and on
her tongue is the law of kindness"

(Proverbs 31:26 NKJV). "May God, who gives this patience and encouragement, help you live in complete harmony with each other" (Romans 15:5 NLT). Gradually, things change with your young stepsister. When you're tempted to speak sharply to her, God's Word comes up out of your heart, saying, "On her tongue is the law of kindness" and "Live in complete harmony with each other." Then you can take a deep breath, smile, and answer in a more gentle manner. Before long, you discover that you actually like your stepsister (and yourself!) much better.

Did You Know ...

the tongue is relatively short at birth, but grows longer (and thinner at the tip) as we get older? Wisdom in how to *use* your tongue needs to grow as well!

Girl Talk:

What things are you tempted to do that you know are wrong? What can you do to change things? Have you worked to change your heart by changing what you feed your mind?

More To Explore: Psalm 37:31 and Proverbs 2:10–11

God Talk:

Lord, you know the problems I have. Help me to change my heart by storing your Word there. Amen.

Devotion #78

"Do you see those who are skilled in their work?
They will serve before kings;
they will not serve before officials of low rank."
—Proverbs 22:29 (TNIV)

Getting a Promotion

Someone who is a trained expert and shows mastery on the job will be promoted. Such a person won't stay under a low-level supervisor. If you want to be promoted, do an excellent job in your work.

When Grace transferred to another school, she immediately joined band. She had been first-chair flute in her old school. But this school was much bigger, and she was placed in the last chair of the flute row. Grace figured that once the band instructor heard her play, he'd move her up to first chair. Only that didn't happen. When he heard her play, he complimented her—but moved her only two seats up the row. At first, Grace was furious. She'd always been the best flute player in band! After her anger died down, however, she admitted that she didn't play as well as those ahead of her. She buckled down and practiced as she'd never practiced before. Slowly, over the course of the year, she moved closer to first chair, being promoted as she grew more skilled.

We all desire promotion, but it doesn't happen just because we want it. We are required to go above and beyond what is asked of us. Whether in school, at home, at a job, on a sports team, or serving in church, being excellent is one key to promotion. "As Jesus grew up, he increased in wisdom and in favor with God and people" (Luke 2:52 TNIV). As we also learn and grow in favor with both God and others, we will rise to the level of promotion God wants for us. Keep a great attitude, and respect and honor those you work under. Then you'll be able to grow in favor with God, who will promote you.

Did You Know ...

David was promoted to serve before a king because he made good use of his God given skills? See 1 Samuel 16:21–23.

Girl Talk:

Are you doing an excellent job at school and at home? Or are you doing only enough to get by?

God Talk:

Lord, help me to do my part— excellent work. And thank you for your part—giving me favor with people. Amen.

More To Explore: 1 Kings 11:28 and Matthew 25:21

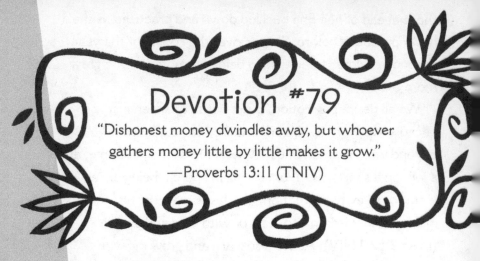

Devotion #79

"Dishonest money dwindles away, but whoever gathers money little by little makes it grow."
—Proverbs 13:11 (TNIV)

Funny Money

Many people try "get rich quick" schemes, things that promise a lot of money with little or no work. Money that is obtained dishonestly includes money received for promising something you don't intend to deliver, blackmail, or money made by trickery. This dishonest money slowly but surely disappears. On the other hand, money made honestly by hard work, saved little by little, will grow.

Suppose you've promised your friends that you'll go to the amusement park, but when it comes to the day of the party, you don't have the money to get in. You don't want to miss it, yet you know there's no point asking your parents for the money. You were supposed to have saved your allowance for the entrance fee, but you spent it on snacks and a new shirt. The night before the party, you dig into your mom's purse and take twenty dollars. It's spent within an hour of entering the park, yet the guilt weighs heavily on you all day. You now wish you'd saved your allowance a little bit every week. Then you could have enjoyed your day at the park. As it is, you're living in dread of your mom discovering the missing money.

Don't let money or the things it can buy become so important that you're willing to get it dishonestly. "Don't try to get rich by extortion or robbery. And if your wealth increases, don't make it the center of your life" (Psalm 62:10 NLT). Then you won't be tempted to obtain money dishonestly. You'll be willing to wait as you work and save, little by little.

Why not open a savings account of your own and start today?

Did You Know ...

a person who gets rich by dishonest means is called "a partridge that hatches eggs it did not lay"? See Jeremiah 17:11.

More To Explore: Psalm 128:1–2

Girl Talk:

Do you have a plan to save part of your allowance or income from jobs such as babysitting? Could you start such a plan?

God Talk:

Lord, I want to be patient and willing to work and save my money. Show me what you want me to do with it. Amen.

Devotion #80

"My soul is weary with sorrow;
strengthen me according to your word."
—Psalm 119:28 (NIV)

Soothe Your Sorrows

Your soul is made up of your mind, your will, and your emotions. When life is difficult, your feelings and body grow weary. Strength to continue comes from God's living and powerful Word.

Sarah envied her friends whose problems consisted of things like finding money for shopping or having a bad hair day. Sarah remembered when those things bothered her too. But ever since her mom got cancer, Sarah had been focused on only one thing. Her mom had had surgery already and was now receiving medicine to kill the remaining cancer cells. Sarah helped out at home after school and on weekends, because her mom was exhausted from the treatments. One night, Sarah cooked supper and folded laundry while trying to memorize facts for her social studies test. Suddenly she was overcome with weariness. Her fears and grief weighed so heavily on her heart. Her tired mind was full of frightening "What-if's?" Leaning on the kitchen counter, Sarah fought the tears that were always near the surface. "Oh, God, help me," she prayed.

That night Sarah crawled into bed with her Bible. She read some verses her pastor had shown her the last time he'd visited the house and talked to them. "I pray that out of [God's] glorious riches he may strengthen you with power through his Spirit in your inner being" (Ephesians 3:16 NIV). Sarah read it out loud three times, then turned to the next one: "I can do everything through [God] who gives me strength" (Philippians 4:13 NIV). She turned off her light and repeated the verse, over and over. Slowly her mind shifted from her mom's cancer to God's power. Finally a sense of calm settled over her, the weariness lifted, and she drifted into a peaceful sleep. She now had strength to carry on.

Did You Know ...

your emotions are created by the thoughts you think? It's true! If you want to feel peaceful, remind yourself to trust God to take care of every situation in your life.

More To Explore: Isaiah 40:31

Girl Talk:

What circumstances make you feel weary and worn out in your mind and emotions? How can God's Word help you transform those feelings?

God Talk:

Lord, sometimes I feel overwhelmed. Thank you for all the help and encouragement in your Word. Amen.

Devotion #81

"Be very careful, then, how you live—
not as unwise but as wise,
making the most of every opportunity,
because the days are evil."
—Ephesians 5:15–16 (NIV)

Capture The Moment!

Show good judgment and common sense by making the most of your time. Don't waste it—you'll never get it back. Control how you spend your time, and be prepared to make the most of every opportunity.

The foolish person has no plan or strategy for her life. She doesn't think ahead and prepare, and so misses many opportunities God might have arranged. "A wise youth works hard all summer; a youth who sleeps away the hour of opportunity brings shame" (Proverbs 10:5 NLT). Opportunity is defined as "a good chance for advancement or progress." All of us desire to get ahead and be promoted in life. However, we must make the necessary preparations before we can go to that next level.

You may know you're too young to get your license yet, but you're intelligent.

You only want the opportunity to drive on country roads where the traffic is light. However, your dad refuses to give you that chance. It would be illegal, and you don't have the necessary skills. Dad won't give you the opportunity to drive a car because you're not prepared for it. In the same way, God withholds opportunities from our lives until we are adequately trained. Even then, an opportunity is just a chance that comes our way. We must walk *through* the doors of opportunity if we desire to fulfill God's plans for our lives. God will send people, ideas, and chances to learn our way. (For example, you could start learning about driving *now*. Study books on driving skills, or watch your parents drive and ask questions.) But if we don't recognize these as opportunities, we won't take advantage of them. Learn to recognize those chances to grow and learn and improve your skills. Take advantage of them. Then you'll be ready and skilled when an opportunity presents itself.

Did You Know ...

Thomas Edison, inventor of the phonograph and lightbulb, once said: "Opportunity is missed by most because it is dressed in overalls and looks like work"?

More To Explore

Ecclesiastes 9:10

Girl Talk:

What opportunities to learn or serve are in front of you right now? What are you going to do with them?

God Talk:

Lord, help me to work hard and grab every opportunity you give me. Thank you for the good future planned for me. Amen.

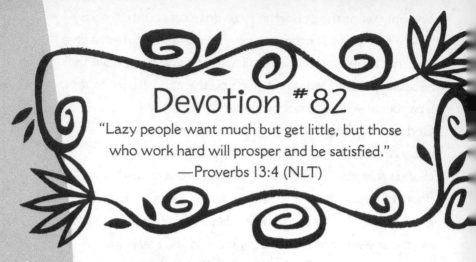

Devotion #82

"Lazy people want much but get little, but those who work hard will prosper and be satisfied."
—Proverbs 13:4 (NLT)

Behold The Sloth

Lazy people (sometimes described as "slothful" in the Bible) prefer not to work or make much effort at physical or mental tasks. They crave (or have a great desire for) many things, yet they refuse to work. People who work hard are the ones who gain wealth and are happy with what they have.

Before her parents divorced, Madison had received a hefty allowance and had few chores to do. She'd grown lazy. She was used to her stay-at-home mom doing all the cooking and cleaning. Now, with her mom working at the office till late, Madison was expected to wash her own laundry and start supper each night after school. At first she hated it. She felt as if she worked all the time. Money was tight, and so her allowance was cut in half. She never had enough money anymore to buy the things she wanted. A full year passed before Madison realized that she could work hard at weekend jobs, save her money, and be able to afford things again.

Some people with laid-back personalities tend to be more lazy, while other people are inclined to be hard workers by nature. Laziness can become a bad habit like any negative behavior. But if that's your problem, you can change! Ask God to help you enjoy working. Your income will increase, and you'll be satisfied with it. "Lazy hands make for poverty, but diligent hands bring wealth" (Proverbs 10:4 TNIV).

Instead of lying around wishing and wanting, decide to overcome your laziness. Work hard—and then be content with what you have earned.

Did You Know ...

the term "slothful" comes from the word *sloth*? A sloth is one of several slow-moving mammals who live in the trees of South America and Central America. They hang from branches and feed on leaves and fruit.

More To Explore: Proverbs 18:9

Girl Talk:

Do you find it easy to be a hard worker or do you tend to be lazy? (Be honest here!) Are there some areas of your life where you work hard, but others where you behave like a sloth?

God Talk:

Lord, I know I need to work harder at some things and not be lazy. Help me to enjoy the results of working hard. Amen.

Devotion #83

"As your words are taught, they give light; even the simple can understand them."

—Psalm 119:130 (NLT)

Turn On The Light!

God's Word isn't complicated. God wrote it so we could understand it and benefit from it. As the Bible is studied and memorized, it sheds light on our confusion. It drives away the darkness.

You're home alone when the electricity is knocked out during a lightning storm. Heart pounding, you crouch in total darkness for a moment. Then you remember the emergency supply of candles and matches in the kitchen drawer. Hands waving in front of you, you grope your way toward the kitchen. You bang your shins on the corner of an end table, hit your hip on the door frame, and slip on the rug in front of the kitchen sink. You're so grateful when you find the candles and matches. After striking a match, you light several candles and place them around the house. No more bruised hips and shins. No more terror. The light pushes back the darkness, showing you where to walk and how to avoid painful encounters.

God's Word is like that. As the principles are studied and put into practice, they give us light to live by. The Bible shows us how to be healthy, how to prosper, how to grow in love for others, and how to avoid dangerous situations. Just like the candles in a dark house, the light of God's Word shows us where to walk and how to avoid painful encounters. "Your word is a lamp to my feet and a light for my path" (Psalm 119:105 NIV). Apart from God's Word, we could only stumble around blindly in the darkness.

Is there an area of your life where you're stumbling in darkness? Then open God's Word, read and study, and be amazed at the light God shines on your problem. Before long, you'll understand what to do.

Did You Know ...

when light waves (which travel in straight lines) encounter any substance, they can either be reflected back or absorbed?

God Talk:

Lord, thank you for giving us your Word. Help me to understand it. Amen.

More To Explore: Proverbs 6:23

Girl Talk:

When you receive the light of God's Word, do you absorb it (and keep it hidden)? Or do you reflect it (and share the light with others)?

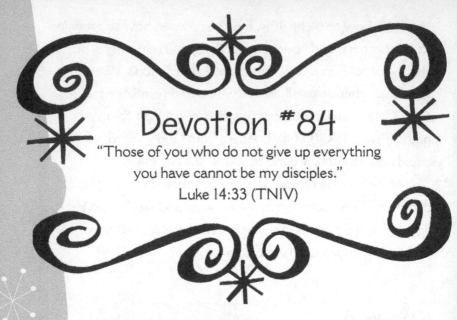

Devotion #84

"Those of you who do not give up everything
you have cannot be my disciples."
Luke 14:33 (TNIV)

Give Up *Every Thing?*

Jesus' words were hard to hear, but he wanted to
warn his followers about the cost of being his disciple.
They'd need to be willing to give up everything, if necessary. Nothing can mean more to a follower of Jesus than
Jesus himself.

Julia had always attended Sunday school and church with
her family, and it was never a problem. But in middle school,
she discovered that several school activities were scheduled
for Sundays. She wanted to play both softball and golf,
but she'd have to skip church to be at the games.

Then, when she applied for a summer job, she
was offered one that required her to work
some Sunday mornings. Julia figured God
would understand if she missed church
sometimes, especially for work or
school activities. Then her mom challenged her, asking what her choice said
about how much she valued her time with

God. Julia faced some difficult decisions.

Every decision you make is proof of what you truly value. Jesus tells us that whoever does not give up everything cannot be his disciple. That's really hard! Does that mean we'll never have anything we want? No. It just means we can't have things (or people) that we value *more* than God. Our actions are a "photograph" of what we value. You may say you value health, but your words mean nothing if you're unwilling to exercise or eat healthy foods.

Are there rewards for giving up everything for Jesus? *Yes!* "No one who has left home or wife or brothers or sisters or parents or children for the sake of the kingdom of God will fail to receive many times as much in this age, and in the age to come eternal life" (Luke 18:29–30 TNIV).

Did You Know ...

when the rich young ruler could not give up his wealth to follow Jesus, the Lord compared the young man to a camel? See Luke 18:22–25.

More To Explore:

Luke 5:11 and I John 2:15

GirL TaLk:

What things do you really value? Does it show in how you spend your time?

God TaLk:

Lord, forgive me for not spending time with you in the past. You do mean everything to me. Amen.

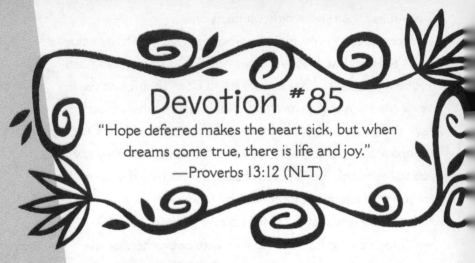

Devotion #85

"Hope deferred makes the heart sick, but when
dreams come true, there is life and joy."
—Proverbs 13:12 (NLT)

Sick at Heart

Most people hope to receive something they really
want. But when their dreams are postponed to a
later time, their hearts become discouraged and disappointed. Yet when those dreams come true, they
bring new life and energy, strengthening them and overcoming their disappointment.

You know firsthand about disappointment. You moved to a
new school when your dad, who's in the U.S. Air Force, was
transferred again. Each day you pray for God to bring a special friend into your life. Every night you cry yourself to
sleep because no one wants to be your friend. You keep
praying. Then one day, you notice the Drama Club's
sign-up sheet on the bulletin board. You love art
and think you could paint scenery. After
school, you meet with the stage crew.
Both Sierra and Jenna are friendly to
you, and the three of you walk home
together afterward. That night, your
disappointment is gone. In its place is a
new joy at having your prayer answered.

We don't always receive what we hope for right away. Just because your answer seems delayed, don't get discouraged and give up praying. Some things just take time. "We want each of you to show this same diligence to the very end, in order to make your hope sure. We do not want you to become lazy, but to imitate those who through faith and patience inherit what has been promised" (Hebrews 6:11–12 NIV).

Keep praying, keep your hope alive—and look forward to a heart filled with joy.

Did You Know ...

in an average lifetime, the heart beats between 2.5 billion and 3 billion times, without ever pausing to rest? Show this same steadiness and reliability while you wait for God to answer your prayers.

More To Explore: Psalm 69:3 and Proverbs 13:19

Girl Talk:

What things are you hoping for that haven't happened yet? Are you still praying for them?

God Talk:

Lord, thank you for putting dreams in my heart. Help me to keep praying— and be patient—while I wait for my dreams to come true. Amen.

Mini Quiz:

If you're discouraged, what can you do to feel better? (Answer "Yes" or "No.")

1. Give the problem to God.
2. Keep thinking about your problems.
3. Pray with thanksgiving.
4. Keep your feelings to yourself.

Answers: 1. Yes [1 Peter 5:7]; 2. No [Philippians 4:6–7]; 3. Yes [Philippians 4:8–9]; 4. No [Psalm 13:1–2]

Devotion #86

"Great peace have they who love your law,
and nothing can make them stumble."
—Psalm 119:165 (NIV)

ChiLL

Complete security and well-being are available for those who study the Bible and live by its principles. If you love the Word with your whole heart—which includes obeying it—then nothing that happens in life can make you falter or trip and fall.

When Jacki moved with her family from a city in the East to a small Midwestern town, she immediately checked out the Dance Club. Jacki had ten years' experience in ballet and had performed in the *Nutcracker Suite* many times. By the time she moved, rehearsals had already begun for the Christmas performance. Jacki observed that none of the girls in lead parts were half as talented as she was. Jacki joined the group that danced in the background, but she burned with jealousy over the "star" part. She was so much better than the stocky girl thudding across the stage! Finally, Jacki could stand it no longer. She talked to the dance instructor. "I don't mean to brag or anything, but I could do a much better job in the lead. I've actually performed with a New York ballet company a few times."

Several girls overheard her, and Jacki feared she'd made a few enemies. Sure enough, girls started avoiding her. She ended up alone—and lonely.

If Jacki had loved God's Word and made it a part of her life—and her actions—she could have avoided stumbling into the "jealousy" and "arrogance" traps. She could have been at peace if she'd acted according to the Scripture: "Love is patient, love is kind and is not jealous; love does not brag and is not arrogant" (1 Corinthians 13:4 NASB).

There's no need to stumble through life, falling down constantly and having to pick yourself up. Instead, learn to love God's laws—and live in peace.

Did You Know ...

just as people who love God's laws will find peace, the opposite is also true? "'There is no peace,' says my God, 'for the wicked'" (Isaiah 57:21 NKJV).

Girl Talk:

Are there areas in your life where you stumble? What verses in the Bible could you apply to bring peace to the situations?

More To Explore: See Philippians 4:6-7

God Talk:

Lord, I don't want to make trouble for myself. Teach me to love your laws. Amen.

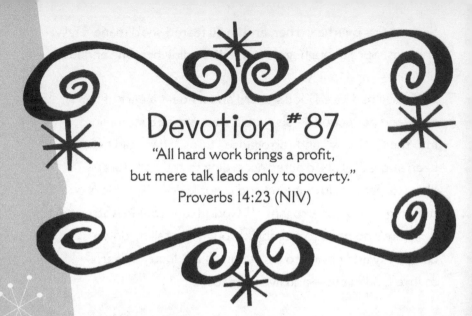

Devotion #87

"All hard work brings a profit,
but mere talk leads only to poverty."
Proverbs 14:23 (NIV)

Talk Is Cheap

If you work hard at anything, there will be a benefit. It might be financial profit or something else to increase your well-being. However, idle chatter leads to having little money or material possessions. Mere talk means little.

You talk all summer about getting fit so you can play basketball in middle school. You read about healthy eating plans and check online fitness websites for training schedules. You plan to be in top shape before tryouts because you've heard running is one test you'll have to pass. You have a great plan for getting in shape. Unfortunately, you never progress beyond talking about it. Putting it into practice looks like hard work. You still go to basketball tryouts in the fall, but you drop out halfway through the required quarter-mile run.

Talk is cheap. It's time to stop being a person who only talks about what she is going to do; it's time to put plans into action. What things have you merely talked about doing for too long? Are you ready to back up your words with activity? Good intentions aren't enough. We must stop expecting to be rewarded for the words we speak. The rewards follow *action*— and usually action that is kept up over a period of time.

It is time to stop talking about "get rich quick" schemes and find a real after-school job. It is time to stop talking about having a deeper relationship with God and start praying more and spending more time in God's Word. We must go beyond knowing what to do and get to a place where we finally do it. "If you know the good you ought to do and don't do it, you sin" (James 4:17 TNIV).

Put those idle words into action—and start reaping the rewards.

Did You Know ...

the Chinese have a proverb about talk being cheap? *Talk does not cook rice.*

God Talk:

Lord, I want to be a person who keeps her word. Help me be someone who doesn't just talk, but puts things into action. Amen.

More To Explore:
Ecclesiastes 5:3

Girl Talk:

What things do you talk about doing—but haven't started or completed yet? Can you take a step today to move from idle chatter to action?

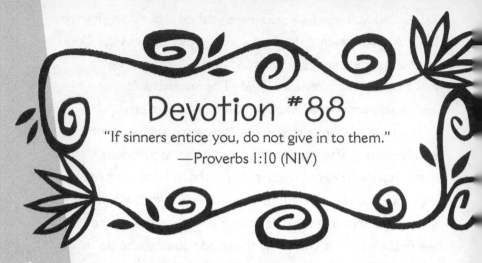

Devotion #88

"If sinners entice you, do not give in to them."
—Proverbs 1:10 (NIV)

Resist The Bait

There will always be people who try to lure or tempt you to do wrong. They make false promises in order to convince you to join them. They try to lure you, much like a fisherman tries to tempt a fish to bite the hook by attaching a brightly colored lure.

Samantha didn't think her friends were sinners or evil people. They just liked to have fun. She had to admit, though, that their idea of fun had changed. Up until sixth grade, they'd all enjoyed hanging at the mall or going skating. Lately, though, her best friend had tried to persuade her to join them in a little bit of shoplifting. "Just a pair of earrings or something small," her friend said. "Nothing expensive. It's just for the thrill of getting away with it. The free jewelry isn't bad either!" She said it was easy, and they never got caught. Samantha knew that shoplifting was wrong, but she didn't want to be left out. The decision was hard. In the end, she chose not to take the bait. She left the mall and took a bus home—alone. She felt both alone and relieved.

How could she avoid having to make that choice in the future? One good way is to not hang out with "friends" who try to coax you into behavior you know is wrong. "Oh, the joys of those who do not follow the advice of the wicked, or stand around with sinners, or join in with scoffers. But they delight in doing everything the LORD wants" (Psalm 1:1–2 NLT). If you don't "stand around with sinners," you are less likely to be swayed to join them in their ungodly and illegal activities.

Don't allow others to coax you off the right path. Be strong, and live for the Lord.

Did You Know ...

the Bible says one kind of ungodly person to avoid is the angry person? (See Proverbs 22:24.) Otherwise, you might become like her.

Girl Talk:

When did someone try to persuade you to join her in doing something wrong? How did you deal with the situation?

More To Explore: Proverbs 13:20

God Talk:

Lord, I know the right thing to do. Help me be determined to do what you want me to do. Amen.

Devotion #89

"I have wandered away like a lost sheep; come and find me, for I have not forgotten your commands."
—Psalm 119:176 (NLT)

Bring Me Back

Sheep can be stupid and wander off into danger-ous places. That's why they need a shepherd to find them, pluck them out of danger, and bring them back to the herd. Jesus is our Good Shepherd. Sometimes, just like dumb sheep, we wander off the path he has for us. He comes and finds us too.

Elizabeth was warned by her dad a dozen times, but she couldn't see any harm in hanging out with her friend's older brother. He was cool, he had a motorcycle, and several times he offered to give her a ride around the block. Ignoring her dad's rule and the warning nudge in her spirit, Elizabeth finally accepted Jason's offer. Thrilled and nervous, she climbed on the back of the motorcycle. What could possibly go wrong in a quick trip around the block? Nothing did—at first. The ride was thrilling! At the second intersection, however, Jason was joking with Elizabeth and pulled out without checking traffic. A car swerved to miss them, but when Jason swerved too, the bike toppled over and slid. Elizabeth's leg was caught underneath, and she left a lot of her skin on the street. Later, when her dad rushed into the emergency room, she turned toward the wall. She couldn't face him.

But her dad just bent over and hugged her. He responded as God does when we wander off temporarily and do stupid things: "I will seek what was lost and bring back what was driven away, bind up the broken and strengthen what was sick" (Ezekiel 34:16 NKJV). If you have wandered away from God in some area of your life, let his Word bring you back home. Let him protect you. "Once you were wandering like lost sheep. But now you have turned to your Shepherd, the Guardian of your souls" (1 Peter 2:25 NLT).

Did You Know ...

the fat from sheep, called tallow, can be used to make both candles and soap?

Girl Talk:

Have you wandered away from the Good Shepherd? Will you *baaaaa* (pray) so he can find you?

God Talk:

Lord, thank you for coming after me when I wander away. Help me to stay close beside you. Amen.

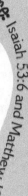

More To Explore Isaiah 53:6 and Matthew 18:12–13

Devotion #90

"I know what it is to be in need, and I know what it is to have plenty. I have learned the secret of being content in any and every situation, whether well fed or hungry, whether living in plenty or in want."
—Philippians 4:12 (NIV)

Happy No Matter What

Paul, a follower of Jesus, said it didn't really matter whether he had many of life's possessions or very few. That isn't where he found his happiness. He had learned to live as happily with nothing as with everything. His joy was in Jesus, not his possessions.

Michelle had plenty of clothes, but she wanted to buy expensive clothes with the "right" labels. She lived in a nice house, but she wanted a fancier one so she could throw lavish parties for her friends. She wasn't happy with what she had. Then, one weekend, her youth group did an activity called "24 Hours in a Box." On a cold night, the group spent the night outside in the parking lot, sleeping in cardboard boxes like the homeless people downtown.

They only had water to drink and a thin blanket for warmth. After a sleepless night, Michelle realized she lived in a palace compared to some people. The next day, she thanked God again and again for a warm house, hot water for a shower, and enough food to eat.

If only I had . . . (you fill in the blank— prettier looks, more athletic skill, better grades, a fancier house, a cell phone or iPod, brand-name clothes). We need to remember that circumstances are not the problem if we're not content. Learn to be happy with your life at this very minute—even if you're working to make it better. How can we learn this contentment? "Take My yoke upon you and learn from Me, for I am gentle and lowly in heart, and you will find rest for your souls. For My yoke is easy and My burden is light" (Matthew 11:29–30 NKJV).

Did You Know ...

the average homeless child in America is only six years old?

God Talk:

Lord, I want to be content. Help me to focus on all the things you've already provided for me instead of wishing for more. Amen.

More To Explore

Girl Talk:

What things do you feel you need in order to be content with your life? Can you learn to be truly happy with less?

2 Corinthians 12:7–10

Devotions

No Boys Allowed Devotions for Girls
Softcover

This short, ninety-day devotional for girls ages 10 and up is written in an upbeat, lively, funny, and tween-friendly way, incorporating the graphic, fast-moving feel of a teen magazine.

Rock Devotions for You
Softcover

In this ninety-day devotional, devotions like "Who Am I?" help pave the spiritual walk of life, and the "Girl Talk" feature poses questions that really bring each message home. No matter how bad things get, you can always count on God.

Chick Chat More Devotions for Girls
Softcover

This ninety-day devotional brings the Bible right into your world and offers lots to learn and think about.

Shine On Girl! Devotions to Keep You Sparkling
Softcover

This ninety-day devotional will "totally" help teen girls connect with God, as well as learn his will for their lives.

NIV Faithgirlz! Bible, Revised Edition

Nancy Rue

Every girl wants to know she's totally unique and special. This Bible says that with Faithgirlz! sparkle. Through the many in-text features found only in the Faithgirlz! Bible, girls will grow closer to God as they discover the journey of a lifetime.

Features include:

- Book introductions—Read about the who, when, where, and what of each book.

- Dream Girl—Use your imagination to put yourself in the story.

- Bring It On!—Take quizzes to really get to know yourself.

- Is There a Little (Eve, Ruth, Isaiah) in You?—See for yourself what you have in common.

- Words to Live By—Check out these Bible verses that are great for memorizing.

- What Happens Next?—Create a list of events to tell a Bible story in your own words.

- Oh, I Get It!—Find answers to Bible questions you've wondered about.

- The complete NIV translation

- Features written by bestselling author Nancy Rue

Available in stores and online!

NIV Faithgirlz! Backpack Bible, Revised Edition

Small enough to fit into a backpack or bag, this Bible can go anywhere a girl does.

Features include:

- Fun Italian Duo-Tone™ design
- Twelve full-color pages of Faithgirlz fun that helps girls learn the "Beauty of Believing!"
- Words of Christ in red
- Ribbon marker
- Complete text of the bestselling NIV translation

Available in stores and online!

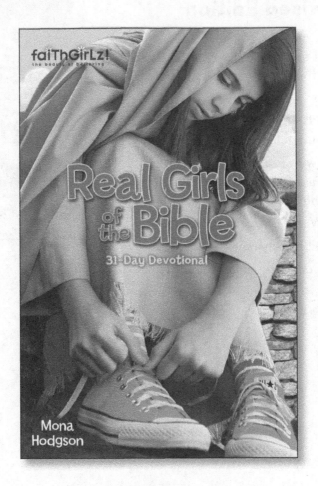